AND GALLOWAY

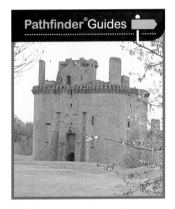

Pathfinder® Guides

Outstanding
Circular Walks

Revised by
Felicity Martin

Text:	Brian Conduit, Hugh Taylor. Revised text for
	2018 edition, Felicity Martin
Photography:	Brian Conduit, Felicity Martin.
	Front cover: © Allan Devlin/Alamy Stock Photo
Editorial:	Ark Creative (UK) Ltd
Design:	Ark Creative (UK) Ltd

This product includes mapping data licensed from Ordnance Survey
© Crown copyright and database rights (2018) OS 150002047

ISBN 978-0-31909-118-0

While every care has been taken to ensure the accuracy of the route directions, the
publishers cannot accept responsibility for errors or omissions, or for changes in details
given. The countryside is not static: hedges and fences can be removed, stiles can be
replaced by gates, field boundaries can be altered, footpaths can be rerouted and
changes in ownership can result in the closure or diversion of some concessionary
paths. Also, paths that are easy and pleasant for walking in fine conditions may
become slippery, muddy and difficult in wet weather, while stepping stones across
rivers and streams may become impassable.

If you find an inaccuracy in either the text or maps, please write to or e-mail
Crimson Publishing at the addresses below.

First published 1997 by Jarrold Publishing and Ordnance Survey.
Revised and reprinted 2005, 2008, 2010. Revised and reprinted by Crimson Publishing
in 2015.

This edition first published in Great Britain 2018 by Crimson Publishing.

Crimson Publishing, 19-21C Charles Street, Bath, BA1 1HX

www.pathfinderwalks.co.uk

Printed in India by Replika Press Pvt. Ltd. 6/18

A catalogue record for this book is available from the British Library.

Front cover: Sweetheart Abbey set against the beautiful backdrop of Criffel
Previous page: Caerlaverock Castle

Contents

Keymaps   4
At-a-glance... walks chart   8
Introduction   10

Walks

1   Doach Wood   16

2   Mull of Galloway   18

3   Water of Ae
Riverside Trail   20

4   Glenkiln   22

5   Caerlaverock and the
Solway Marshes   24

6   Wigtown   27

7   Moffat Well and
Gallow Hill   30

8   Lochmaben and
the Four Lochs   32

9   Up and Down
the Annan   35

10   Fleet Forest and
Anwoth Old Kirk   38

11   Wanlockhead and
Lowther Hill   41

12   Water of Luce
and Kilhern   44

13   Rascarrel Bay and
Balcary Point   46

14   Screel Hill   48

15   Water of Ken and
Garroch Glen   50

16   Devil's Beef Tub   53

17   Loch Trool   56

18   St Ninian's Cave and
Burrow Head   59

19   Manquhill Hill   62

20   Portpatrick and
Killantringan Fell   64

21   Mabie Forest   67

22   Cairnsmore of Dee   70

23   Sweetheart Abbey
and Criffel   72

24   Cairnsmore of Fleet   75

25   Black Hill and Well Hill   78

26   Caldons Burn and
Lamachan Hill   81

27   Colvend Coast   84

28   Merrick   88

Further Information   92

Walkers and the Law;
Glossary of Gaelic Names;
Safety on the Hills;
Useful Organisations;
Ordnance Survey Maps

Approximate walk times

Up to 3 hours
Short walks on generally
clear paths

2 ½-4 hours
Slightly harder walks of
moderate length

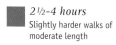

4 hours and over
Longer walks including
some steep ascents/
descents occasionally on
faint paths

*The walk times are provided as a guide only and are calculated using an average walking
speed of 2½mph (4km/h), adding one minute for each 10m (33ft) of ascent, and then rounding
the result to the nearest half hour.*

GIRVAN

SCALE 1:312 500 or 1 INCH to 5 MILES *1CM to 3.1 KM*

0 2 4 6 8 10 KILOMETRES 15

0 2 4 6 MILES 8 10

SPOT HEIGHTS SHOWN IN METRES

Woodland Bay
Byne
Saugh Hill 296
Mull of Miljoan 355
Glengennet
Tormitchell

B734

Lendalfoot
Knockdaw Hill
260
187
236
Mid Hill
411
479
Greensides 335
Pindonnan Craigs

Bennane Head
Colmonell
Knockdolian
266
Castle
Pinwherry
Poundland
227
Bellamore

BALLANTRAE BAY

Knockdolian
59
Heronsford
230
Glen Tig
Knockdhu
Pinwherry Hill
Barrhill
73

Ballantrae
Cosses
Baldissock
Shiel Hill
Corwar House

Downan Point
Glenapp Castle
Smyrton
Benerard
317

Currarie Port
Carlock Hill
319
164
Miljoan Hill
403
Strawarren Fell
Chirmorrie
195
Drumlamford Loch
Drumlamford House

Penderry Hill
High Murdonochee

Milleur Point
Stab Hill
221
Miltonise
287
Craig Airie Fell
185
Polbae
Loch Maberry

Barnhills
Portencalzie
99
Mid Moile
257
Penwhirn Reservoir
Standing Stones
Urrall Fell
184

North Cairn
Glen APP
19
Quarter Fell
254
Eldrig Fell
226

Corsewall
Cairn Point
Lamb Hill
238
Artfield Fell
Loch Ochiltree

Knockcoid
Kirkcolm
The Wig
96
CAIRNRYAN
Braid Fell
Balmurrie
Loch Moan

Ervie
Kirminnoch
St Mary's Croft
A77
Cairnscarrow
New Luce
12
Loch Ronald

Knocknain
Leswalt
LOCH RYAN
Auchmantle
Drumphail
205
Bught Fell

Lochnaw Castle
B7043
Innermessan
Lochinch Castle
Craig Fell
164
Gleniron Fell
Whitecairn
Carscreugh
Barlae
Craighlaw

Glenstockadale
A718
STRANRAER
Aird
White Loch
Black Loch
Abbey
Dergoals
98
Dernaglar Loch

Portslogan
Southern Upland Way
A77
Castle Kennedy
Challoch Hill
148
Dunragit
A75
Glenluce
Knock Moss

Black Head
Craigenlee Fell
109
Whiteleys Lochans
182
Cairn Pat
Genoch Mains
B7077
Torrs Warren
Milton
Whitefield Loch
131

20
Dunskey Castle
A77
A716
Bean Hill
Collin
Luce Sands
Stairhaven
Auchenmalg
A747

Port of Spittal Bay
B7042
Awhirk
Stoneykirk
Craignarget Hill
Doon of May
Altic ry
Culshaw
Mochrum

Cairngarroch Bay
Money Head
Meikle Float
Cairngarroch
Sandhead
Chapel Finian
Milton Point

Float Bay
Hole Stone Bay
Clachanmore
Ardwell
Chapel Rossan Bay

Ardwell Mains
Ardwell Point
Logan Mains
A716
Balgowan Point
L U C E   B A Y

Mull of Logan
Logan
Terally Point

Port Nessock or Port Logan Bay
Cairnywellan Head
Port Logan
B7065
122
Kilstay Bay

Clanyard Bay
Clanyard
Kirkmaiden
Drummore
Cailness Point

Laggantalluch Head
Damnaglaur
164
Maryport
Maryport Bay
Scares

Crammag Head
161

Cairngaan
Port Kemin
MULL OF GALLOWAY
2

28 **17** **26** **19** **15** **22** **24** **6** **10** **18**

CARRICK FOREST
GLENTROOL FOREST
MERRICK
KIRROUGHTREE FOREST
GLENGAP FOREST
LAURIESTON FOREST
CAIRNSMORE OF FLEET
THE MACHARS
GALLOWAY
THE GLENKENS
RHINNS OF KELLS

Carsphairn
Glenhoul
St John's Town of Dalry
NEW GALLOWAY
Balmaclellan
Ironmacannie
Bogue
Earlstoun
Mossdale
Little Duchrae
Laur
Ringford
Twynholm
KIRKCUDBRIGHT
St Mary's Isle
Dund
Townhead
Balmae
Nether
Brighouse Bay
Little Ross
Borness Point

Gatehouse of Fleet
Anwoth
Cardoness
Girthon
Sandgreen
Knockbrex
Mile-end
Borgue
Kirkandrews
Borness
Brighouse Ross

NEWTON STEWART
Minnigaff
Cumloden
Boreland
Challoch
Glenrazie
Calgow
Stronord
Palnure
Benfield
Barraer Fell
Barraer
High Moor of Killiemore
Battersan
Causeway End
Carsegowan
Spittal
Torhousemuir
Stone Circle
WIGTOWN
Bladnoch
Braehead
Kirkinner
Whauphill
Barrachan
Airyhassen
Mochrum
Drumroddan Rocks
Big Balcraig
Monreith Mains
Sorbie
Garlieston
Eggerness Point
Innerwell Port
Cults
Castlewigg
Priory
Fell of Barrhullion
Monreith
WHITHORN
Glasserton
Fell of Carleton
St Ninian's Cave
Tonderghie
Isle of Whithorn
St Ninian's Chapel
Cairn Head
Portyerrock Bay
Port Allen
Port Castle Bay
BURROW HEAD
Point of Cairndoon

WIGTOWN BAY
Wigtown Sands
Baldoon Sands
Carsluith
Carsluith Castle
Ravenshall Point
Fleet Bay
Islands of Fleet

Creetown
Glen
Culcronchie
Pibble Hill
Stey Fell
Cairnharrow
Cairndely
Bengray
Loch Whinyeon
Lochenbreck Loch
White Top of Culreoch
Airie Hill
Craiglowrie
Loch Skerrow
Shaw Hill
Fell of Fleet
Clints of Dromore
Cairnsmore
Knocknevis
Round Fell
Dunkitterick Cottage
Craignelder
Auchinleck
Garlies Castle
Bruce's Stone
Loch Grannoch
Black Water of Dee

Cairnsmore of Fleet
Loch Dee
Loch Trool
Buchan
Glentrool Village
Bargrennan
Glenamour
Glencaird Hill
Garwall Hill
Larg Hill
Lamachan Hill
Garlick Hill
Auchinleck

CARRICK FOREST
Eldrick Hill
Black Hill
Craiglee
Craigmalloch
Loch Doon Castle
Loch Recar
Loch Macaterick
Macaterick
Tarfessock
Kirriereoch Hill
Mullwharchar
Corserine
Round Loch of the Dungeon
Loch Enoch
Loch Neldricken
Loch Valley
Benyellary
Merrick

Lamford Hill
Dodd Hill
Brochloch
Carsphairn
Cairn Avel
Bardennoch
Castlemaddy
Thorny Hill
Forrest Lodge
Knocknalling
Drumbuie
Garros
Glenlee
Mid Garrary
Craigencallie House
Cairngarroch
Darnaw
Brockloch Hill
Knocknevis
Bennan
Corriedoo
Culmark Hill
Marscalloch Hill
Knowehead
Kendoon Loch
Earlshagg Loch
Loch Harrow
Loch Dungeon
Meikle Millyea
Little Duchrae
Stroan Loch
Woodhall Loch
Mannoch
Benbrack
Cairn Edward Hill
Kenmure Castle
Loch Ken

A713 A762 A712 A75 A714 A746 A747 A711 A755 A71 A702 B729 B7000 B7027 B796 B794 B7004 B7052 B7005 B7085

Keymap 2

SCALE 1:312 500 or 1 INCH to 5 MILES 1CM to 3.1 KM

KILOMETRES
0 2 4 6 8 10 12 14 15

MILES
0 2 4 6 8 10

SPOT HEIGHTS SHOWN IN METRES

11

25

19

15

4

1

14

27

10

13

SANQUHAR

THORNHILL

MONIAIVE

ST JOHN'S TOWN OF DALRY

NEW GALLOWAY

CROCKETFORD

CASTLE DOUGLAS

DALBEATTIE

KIRKCUDBRIGHT

GATEHOUSE OF FLEET

DUNDRENNAN

AUCHENCAIRN

Kirkconnel

New

Mennock

A76

A702

A712

A713

A762

A75

A711

A710

A745

A794

DALMACALLAN FOREST

LAURIESTON FOREST

GLENGAP FOREST

DALBEATTIE FOREST

Southern Upland Way

Balcary Point

Hestan Island

Castlehill Point

Mersehead

Islands of Fleet

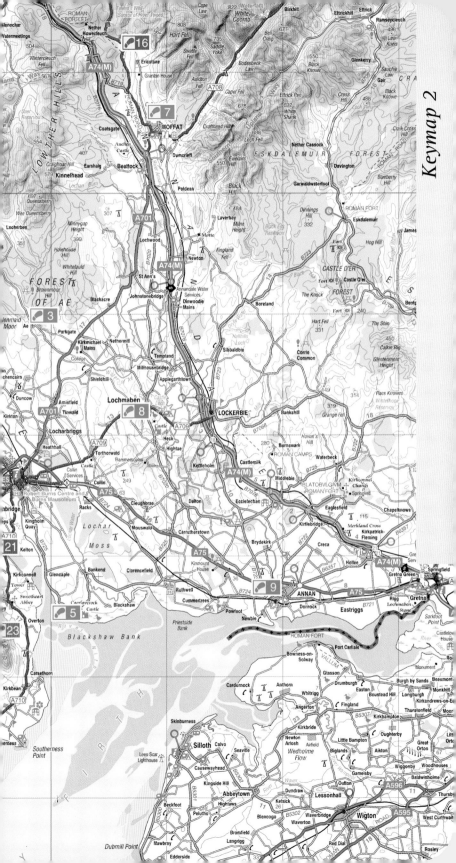

Keymap 2

At-a-glance

Walk	Page	Start	Nat. Grid Reference	Distance	Time	Height Gain
Black Hill and Well Hill	78	Durisdeer	NS 893037	5½ miles (8.9km)	4 hrs	1,855ft (565m)
Caerlaverock and the Solway Marshes	24	Castle Wood Car Park	NY 019652	3½ miles (5.6km)	1¾ hrs	310ft (95m)
Cairnsmore of Dee	70	Clatteringshaws Loch	NX 551762	6 miles (9.7km)	4 hrs	1,705ft (520m)
Cairnsmore of Fleet	75	Cairnsmore Estate car park	NX 463632	7½ miles (12.2km)	4½ hrs	2,295ft (700m)
Caldons Burn and Lamachan Hill	81	Bridge over the River Trool	NX 397791	8½ miles (13.7km)	5½ hrs	2,380ft (725m)
Colvend Coast	84	Kippford	NX 836553	10 miles (16.1km)	5 hrs	835ft (255m)
Devil's Beef Tub	53	Devil's Beef Tub	NT 062125	5½ miles (8.9km)	3 hrs	740ft (225m)
Doach Wood	16	Doach Wood	NX 793577	2½ miles (4km)	1½ hrs	280ft (85m)
Fleet Forest and Anwoth Old Kirk	38	Gatehouse of Fleet	NX 599561	5½ miles (8.9km)	2½ hrs	360ft (110m)
Glenkiln	22	Glenkiln Reservoir	NX 839784	3½ miles (5.6km)	1¾ hrs	295ft (90m)
Loch Trool	56	Bridge over the River Trool	NX 397791	5½ miles (8.9km)	3 hrs	475ft (145m)
Lochmaben and the Four Lochs	32	Lochmaben	NY 080826	5½ miles (8.9km)	2½ hrs	130ft (40m)
Mabie Forest	67	Mabie Forest	NX 949710	7¼ miles (11.6km)	4 hrs	1,295ft (395m)
Manquhill Hill	62	Stroanpatrick	NX 643917	6¾ miles (10.6km)	3½ hrs	900ft (275m)
Merrick	88	Bruce's Stone, Loch Trool	NX 415804	9⅛ miles (15.3km)	6½ hrs	2,575ft (785m)
Moffat Well and Gallow Hill	30	Moffat	NT 084054	4 miles (6.4km)	2 hrs	330ft (100m)
Mull of Galloway	18	Mull of Galloway	NX 154304	3 miles (4.8km)	1½ hrs	375ft (115m)
Portpatrick and Killantringan Fell	64	Portpatrick	NW 998542	8 miles (12.9km)	4 hrs	1,380ft (420m)
Rascarrel Bay and Balcary Point	46	Balcary Bay	NX 821494	5 miles (8km)	2½ hrs	310ft (95m)
Screel Hill	48	Screel Wood	NX 800546	3½ miles (5.6km)	2½ hrs	1,085ft (330m)
St Ninian's Cave and Burrow Head	59	Kidsdale	NX 431366	7½ miles (12.1km)	3½ hrs	475ft (145m)
Sweetheart Abbey and Criffel	72	New Abbey	NX 964663	6½ miles (10.5km)	4½ hrs	2,015ft (615m)
Up and Down the Annan	35	Annan	NY 191666	6½ miles (10.5km)	3 hrs	N/a
Wanlockhead and Lowther Hill	41	Wanlockhead	NS 873129	4½ miles (7.2km)	2½ hrs	1,015ft (310m)
Water of Ae Riverside Trail	20	Ae Forest car park	NX 984894	3½ miles (5.6km)	1½ hrs	150ft (45m)
Water of Ken and Garroch Glen	50	St John's Town of Dalry	NX 619812	4½ miles (7.2km)	2½ hrs	510ft (155m)
Water of Luce and Kilhern	44	New Luce	NX 174647	5½ miles (8.9km)	2½ hrs	345ft (105m)
Wigtown	27	Wigtown	NX 433552	4½ miles (7.2km)	2 hrs	280ft (85m)

Comments

There are fine views over Nithsdale and the Lowther Hills but expect some steep and rough climbing on the first part of this walk.

For a short walk there is an immense amount of interest: splendid medieval castle, fine woodland, coastal marshes and superb views from the earthworks of a prehistoric fort.

Despite a height of only 1,616ft (493m), the latter part of this climb to the summit of Cairnsmore of Dee is very rough going. The views across Clatteringshaws Loch are outstanding.

The easiest of all the hill climbs in this guide. Pick a clear day and enjoy the superb views on both the ascent and descent.

A mixture of difficult paths – muddy and rocky – beside Caldons Burn and clear forest tracks. The extensive views from the higher points are superb.

An outstanding walk along one of the finest stretches of the Solway coast is complemented by attractive forested sections on the return leg.

The walk takes you around the edge of a deep and dramatic natural depression at the head of Annandale.

A short and easy climb through an impressive collection of Douglas firs brings you to a fine view-point overlooking the Solway.

A contrasting walk: attractive woodland on the first half; open, heathery moorland on the second, with a descent to a ruined church.

A gentle walk amid the lovely scenery of Glenkiln overlooking the reservoir. Formerly a sculpture park, Glenkiln Cross by Henry Moore can still be seen on the skyline.

This circuit of Loch Trool in the heart of the Galloway Forest Park gives magnificent views over the surrounding mountains, including glimpses of Merrick.

This walk takes in the four lochs that surround Lochmaben and includes a visit to the ruined former castle of the Bruces.

From the forested slopes above the River Nith there are fine views of Criffel and across the Nith Estuary and Solway coast.

A lonely walk with a real sense of remoteness that reveals the austere and empty landscape of the Southern Uplands at its best.

Choose a fine day and take your time. This is a lengthy and demanding walk but standing on the highest point in southern Scotland gives immense satisfaction.

Enjoy fine views of Annandale and the surrounding hills. The final stretch of the walk is a descent through lovely woodland.

Rugged cliff scenery is enjoyed on this easy circuit of the Mull of Galloway, the most southerly point in the whole of Scotland.

The first few miles of the Southern Upland Way is followed on this spectacular coastal walk. There are several climbs.

Some fine cliff scenery and grand views across the Solway are the highlights of this walk. Note that the path around Balcary Point is steep and exposed in places.

A steady climb through woodland leads to the summit of Screel Hill above the Solway which, despite its modest height, is a magnificent all-round viewpoint.

A beautiful wooded valley leads to the coast by St Ninian's Cave and this is followed by some superb cliff-top walking.

A beautiful ruined abbey is the start of this long, steady climb to the summit of one of the most distinctive peaks in Dumfries and Galloway.

There is attractive scenery all the way on this walk beside the River Annan from Annan to Brydekirk and back.

As well as grand views over lonely hills, there is much of interest in the former lead-mining village of Wanlockhead, the highest village in Scotland.

A lovely riverside walk beside the lively Water of Ae, winding between giant Norway spruce, and with many wildlife- and birdlife-spotting opportunities.

There are outstanding views over the Ken valley from the Southern Upland Way on the latter part of the walk.

A walk along narrow lanes and across open moorland, with dramatic views over the valley of the Water of Luce.

There are superb views across the wide expanses of Wigtown Bay and the Bladnoch Estuary to the bold outlines of the Galloway Hills.

Introduction to Dumfries and Galloway

Dumfries and Galloway is Scotland's south west, a broad wedge of land jutting out into the Irish Sea between the Solway Firth and the Firth of Clyde. It is also part of Scotland's border country; from the higher points of the Galloway hills the mountains of the English Lake District can be seen rising above the opposite shores of the Solway and, in clear conditions, the hills of Northern Ireland are also visible on the skyline. Lying between the Highlands to the north and the Lake District mountains to the south, Dumfries and Galloway can get overlooked by many hill walkers and tourists, but for those sensible enough to stop and explore, the reward is a peaceful, unspoilt region that possesses a mild climate, tremendously varied scenery and a rich historic legacy.

Mountains, forests and lochs
Most walkers will perhaps head for the hills and mountains of the Southern Uplands that sweep across the region before continuing eastwards into the Borders. The mountains of Dumfries and Galloway offer plenty of remote and challenging walking and there are over 40 peaks that exceed 2,000 feet. The highest of these, and indeed the highest point in southern Scotland, is Merrick (2,766ft/843m). The ascent of Merrick, described in *Walk 28*, is no

On the Southern Uplands Way near the Water of Ken

The descent from Merrick

mean feat and many will find it more strenuous and difficult than that of some higher peaks in other parts of the country.

On no account must the Galloway hills be underestimated. A change in the weather or decline in visibility can prove dangerous, and with often difficult conditions underfoot and a lack of landmarks, they should not be tackled in bad weather by any but the experienced and properly equipped. Even on the lower slopes there is often rough walking across heather, bracken and rocks with burns to ford, and few of the hills, apart from Merrick, Cairnsmore of Fleet and Criffel, have clearly defined paths leading to their summits.

The main Galloway hills can be divided into six ranges: Merrick is one of the 'fingers' that constitute 'The Awful Hand' range, so called because the individual peaks are spread out like the fingers and thumb of a hand. This is the most westerly of three parallel north-south ranges; the other two are Dungeon and the Rhinns of Kells. To the south of these is the Minnigaff group, which includes Lamachan Hill, and to the north east is the lofty Carsphairn range. The final, more scattered, range is the Solway hills that stretch from Cairnsmore of Fleet overlooking Wigtown Bay to Criffel overlooking the Nith Estuary.

Chief characteristics of the Southern Uplands are sweeping, grassy slopes rather than crags and jagged profiles, and in Dumfries and Galloway many of the lower slopes are covered by extensive conifer plantations. In the heart of the region is the Galloway Forest Park: over 300 square miles (777 sq km) of forest and moorland, mountains and lochs; a haven for wildlife with miles of waymarked trails. Farther east is the Forest of Ae, and many other forests – Dalbeattie and Mabie – extend southwards to the Solway coast, all of them offering excellent walking opportunities.

Complementing the landscape of mountains and forests is the multitude of lochs of all sizes, both natural and man-made. One of the most beautiful, and certainly the most popular, of these is Loch Trool in the heart of the Forest Park, closely associated with Robert Bruce's successful struggles to preserve Scottish independence. The paths that encircle it, featured in Walk 17, are outstandingly attractive.

Coastline, valleys and marshes

Away from the hills some of the most enjoyable and spectacular walking is to be found along the long and heavily indented coastline of the Solway Firth and Irish Sea. It is a varied coast with flat and marshy land at the eastern end of the Solway rising to impressively rugged cliffs farther west.

Newton Stewart

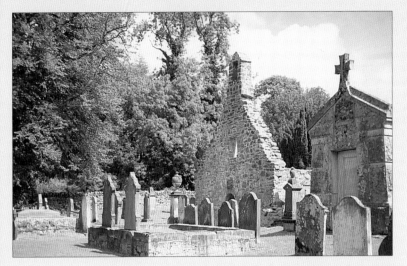

Anwoth Old Kirk

There is particularly fine walking along the Solway, between Kippford and Sandyhills *(Walk 27)*, around the southern tips of the two long peninsulas of the Machars *(Walk 18)* and the Rhinns of Galloway *(Walk 2)*, and along the west coast north of Portpatrick *(Walk 20)*, the start of the Southern Upland Way.

Although there is an inevitable emphasis on hills and mountains, forests and coast, there are also several pleasant lowland walks. The wide lower valleys of the Rivers Nith and Annan, the marshes of the Solway coast, and the flat expanses of the 'debatable lands' just across the English border all provide contrasting walking for those who prefer something easier and more relaxing.

Historic heritage

Dumfries and Galloway has played a major role in some of the most momentous events in Scottish history. Scottish Christianity was born here when St Ninian established the first church in Scotland at Whithorn in AD397. Later, a monastery was built on the site which became the cathedral of the medieval bishops of Galloway. Parts of this church survive, and two nearby sites also associated with St Ninian are the ruined chapel at Isle of Whithorn and St Ninian's Cave, the latter featured in *Walk 18*.

In the late 17th century the area became one of the main centres of the Covenanters Movement. The Covenanters were Presbyterians who rejected bishops and refused to accept the king as head of the Church. Many of them were persecuted and executed for their beliefs and both *Walks 6* and *16* pass memorials to these martyrs.

It was among the lochs and hills of Dumfries and Galloway that Robert Bruce began the struggle to maintain Scottish independence against the ambitions of Edward I of England. The eastern part is border country and English invaders regularly used the valleys of the Nith and Annan as routeways into Scotland. The castles at Annan *(Walk 9)* and Lochmaben *(Walk 8)* were strongholds of the Bruce family and Robert Bruce's victories are commemorated at various spots throughout the region. Most notable of these is the Bruce Stone, that occupies a magnificent position overlooking Loch Trool.

The chief town of the region is Dumfries, associated with one of the most famous of Scottish literary figures. Robert Burns lived the last years of his life in the town and is buried in St Michael's church there. The other towns – Castle Douglas, Newton Stewart, Kirkcudbright, Wigtown, Moffat – are mainly small market towns and tourist centres.

Routes and weather

In Dumfries and Galloway there is plenty of variety and a wide range of walking routes to suit all ages, aptitudes and levels of fitness. Many of the walks in this guide make use of stretches of the well-waymarked Southern Upland Way, the only national trail in the region, that begins its 212 mile (340km) journey across Scotland on the west coast of Galloway. Others use hill, coastal, lochside and riverside paths and the many forest trails.

Like the other west-facing peninsulas of Britain – Cornwall, Wales, Cumbria – Dumfries and Galloway has a generally mild climate but also has its fair share of rain. Probably the best months for dry weather and sunny conditions are from April to June, but walking here is a joy at all seasons of the year. Simply choose the walk that is best suited both to your own requirements and fitness and the prevailing weather conditions, taking particular notice of the latter if you are venturing on to some of the higher hills.

Loch Trool

Important note
It must be stressed that although of immense scenic and

Portpatrick

recreational value, the forests of Dumfries and Galloway were planted mainly for commercial reasons and at certain times felling operations may cause the temporary closure and re-routing of some of the trails. Whenever this occurs, Forestry Commission notices will be posted at the start of the affected walks.

This book includes a list of waypoints alongside the description of the walk, so that you can enjoy the full benefits of gps should you wish to.
For more information on using your gps, read the *Pathfinder® Guide GPS for Walkers*, by gps teacher and navigation trainer, Clive Thomas (ISBN 978-0-7117-4445-5). For essential information on map reading and basic navigation, read the *Pathfinder® Guide Map Reading Skills* by outdoor writer, Terry Marsh (ISBN 978-0-7117-4978-8). Both titles are available in bookshops or can be ordered online at www.pathfinderwalks.co.uk

Doach Wood

		GPS waypoints
Start	Doach Wood, off B736 3 miles (4.8km) south-east of Castle Douglas	📝 NX 793 577
		Ⓐ NX 142 310
Distance	2½ miles (4km)	Ⓑ NX 143 308
Height gain	280 feet (85m)	Ⓒ NX 798 579
Approximate time	1½ hours	
Parking	Forestry Commission car park at Doach Wood	
Ordnance Survey maps	Landranger 84 (Dumfries & Castle Douglas), Explorer 313 (Dumfries & Dalbeattie)	

There are two main attractions on this short walk: the fine viewpoint along the Solway coast from the highest point and the magnificent collection of Douglas firs, especially on the latter stages. All the ascents and descents are gradual, the route is easy to follow, and the tracks and paths are firm and well-drained so that there are few muddy stretches even after prolonged rain.

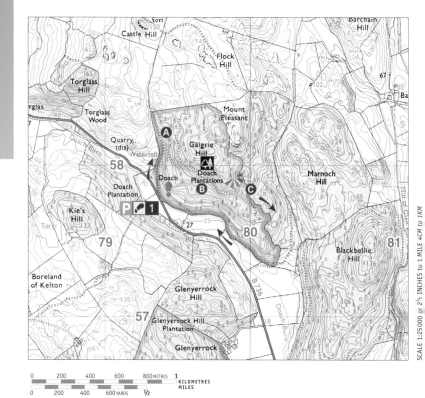

Doach Wood

🖋 Facing the wood turn left, pass beside a gate and take the steadily ascending track uphill to reach a hairpin bend. Follow the track to the right around the bend **A** and continue uphill.

At the top turn left and head up a faint track on the banking to reach another footpath. Turn uphill **B** by a yellow waymarker then keep on up the hill to reach the viewpoint **C**.

A 'Solway View' board indicates all of the many places that can be seen on a clear day from here. These include: Hestan Island, Bengairn, Screel Hill and the mountains of the English Lake District.

Retrace your steps to the track **B** and turn left, now following yellow-topped posts for the remainder of the walk. Head gently downhill, later curving gradually to the right. The track narrows to a path which winds more steeply downhill, going round some sharp bends. On this part of the walk the Douglas firs are most impressive and there are views of the wooded slopes of Glenyerrock Hill across fields to the left as the path continues along the bottom inside edge of the wood.

After a path junction, where you keep straight on, there is a particularly fine display of Douglas firs on the steep hillside to the right. The path leads directly back to the car park. ●

Mull of Galloway

		GPS waypoints
Start	Mull of Galloway, where road ends at the tip of the Rhinns of Galloway	✏ NX 154 304
Distance	3 miles (4.8km)	Ⓐ NX 142 310
Height gain	375 feet (115m)	Ⓑ NX 143 308
Approximate time	1½ hours	Ⓒ NX 155 306
Parking	Mull of Galloway	
Ordnance Survey maps	Landranger 82 (Stranraer & Glenluce), Explorer 309 (Stranraer & The Rhins)	

The Mull of Galloway, situated at the tip of the peninsula of the Rhinns of Galloway and almost detached from it, is Scotland's most southerly point. It is said that from it you can see five kingdoms – Scotland, England, Ireland, Isle of Man, and the Kingdom of Heaven. You can certainly see some majestic cliffs on this short and easy walk, which for the most part keeps along the edge of the cliffs. This walk is best avoided by vertigo sufferers, and in such an exposed location, it is best to avoid this walk on windy days.

Spectacular cliffs, Mull of Galloway

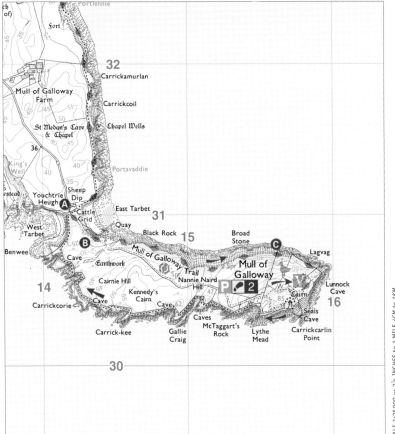

0	200	400	600	800 METRES 1

KILOMETRES
MILES

0   200   400   600 YARDS   ½

Begin by going through the gate into the nature reserve. Walk along the tarmac path and then at a junction turn left onto the circular route. This will take you to the RSPB Visitor Centre which is housed in the building once used by the men who built the lighthouse in 1828.

Continue past the visitor centre towards the lighthouse. Turn right and follow the tarmac path back to the car park. Cross the car park to the **Gallie Craig Coffee House** and turn left through a kissing-gate in front of it to access the path along cliffs, passing Gallie Craig, the southernmost point in Scotland. Because of the narrowness of the peninsula, the coast is seen to both left and right. Curve to the right to reach

the neck of the peninsula – literally only a few yards wide – and by a cattle-grid turn right **A** along the road.

You can follow the road back to the car park, but for a more scenic alternative turn left **B** down a track (Mull of Galloway Trail) to the attractive bay of East Tarbet, pass a cottage then climb up to the fence on the right and continue around the shore on a rougher path between it and the cliffs.

On reaching the boundary of the nature reserve **C**, turn right through a gate and walk alongside the wall to return to the start.

Water of Ae Riverside Trail

		GPS waypoints
Start	Ae Forest	📛 NX 984 894
Distance	3½ miles (5.6km)	Ⓐ NX 983 901
Height gain	150 feet (45m)	Ⓑ NX 981 907
Approximate time	1½ hours	Ⓒ NX 981 911
Parking	Ae Forest car park (Pay & Display)	Ⓓ NX 984 915
Ordnance Survey maps	Landranger 78 Nithsdale & Annandale area Explorer 321 Nithsdale & Dumfries	

The Water of Ae Riverside Trail runs beside a lively river and weaves between the trunks of gigantic Norway spruce. Red squirrels, dippers and many species of woodland birds abound here. This central part of the Forest of Ae, a vast conifer plantation north of Dumfries, is laid out with recreational trails for walkers, horse riders and cyclists. It is one of the five 7stanes mountain biking centres in Dumfries & Galloway, and the outward and return path is shared with cyclists.

📛 Start beside a 7Stanes mountain biking information board and leave the car park on a path with an ornamental wooden fence beside it, following yellow waymarked posts. Soon turn right on a track that leads to a junction and here turn left along a dirt lane. After crossing a cattle grid, you can walk parallel to the lane through the grassy field on the right if you wish to avoid cars coming and going from the overspill car park ahead.

At the edge of the conifer forest Ⓐ, turn left then take the second right through the overspill car park to a 7stanes information point. Keep ahead on a shared-use path running beside the Water of Ae. Come to a sculpted bench with carved wildlife figures, which commemorates the founding of Ae forest village in 1947. Here turn left across a bridge over the Water of

Ae Ⓑ then go immediately right to continue upstream on the other side of the river. Keep a look out for white-chested dippers bobbing on rocks or plunging under the water in search of insect larvae. Deciduous trees line the river and several crab apples overhang the path – a particularly lovely sight in spring and autumn.

Follow the path as it bends away from the river, crosses a forest road, and comes to a junction Ⓒ. Turn right here and at the next junction keep left. The path now runs under big Norway spruce with tall, straight trunks. By a little pond, a grassy area opens up on the left. Around this are arranged a display of historic forestry ploughs, many of which were designed and made by the nearby machinery company Clarks of Parkgate. Here re-cross the forest road and turn right

Memorial bench to the establishment of Ae Forest village in 1947

passing under more towering Norway spruce. Once again cross the forest road and at a junction turn left along a track back to the bridge (there are mountain bike trails to the right). Re-cross the bridge **B** and turn right by the carved bench, then retrace your steps back via the overspill car park and dirt lane to the main car park. ●

D on a path to return beside the fast flowing Water of Ae.

After crossing the forest road again, go left at a path junction along a section of the outward route. At the next junction **C**, keep straight ahead,

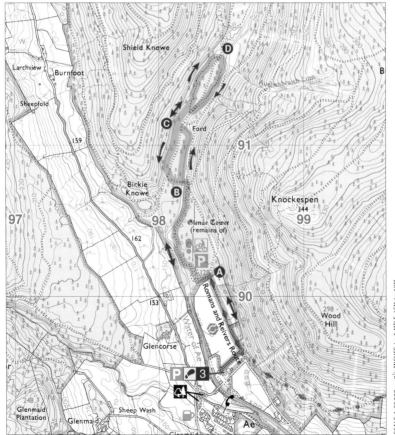

Glenkiln

Start	Glenkiln Reservoir, on minor road north-west of Shawhead	
Distance	3½ miles (5.6km)	
Height gain	295 feet (90m)	
Approximate time	1¾ hours	
Parking	Car park just beyond north end of Glenkiln Reservoir	
Ordnance Survey maps	Landranger 84 (Dumfries & Castle Douglas), Explorer 321 (Nithsdale & Dumfries)	

GPS waypoints

- ✐ NX 839 784
- Ⓐ NX 842 780
- Ⓑ NX 850 772
- Ⓒ NX 837 767

This walk became famous because the local landowner erected a series of works by well-known sculptors around the route: Moore, Epstein and Rodin. Unfortunately one was stolen and most were then removed to safe storage. Moore's Glenkiln Cross can still be seen on the skyline high above the road – it's a great viewpoint if you have the energy to walk up to it. Although not graced with so many artworks, the scenery around Glenkiln Reservoir is still lovely.

✐ Begin by turning left out of the car park along the lane beside Glenkiln Reservoir, which was created in 1934 to supply drinking water to Dumfries and surrounding areas. Moore's *Glenkiln Cross* can be seen in a commanding position on the hill to the right, and a metal gate on the right Ⓐ, just before a passing place, enables you to detour up to it for the superb view over the reservoir. Continue past the end of the reservoir, heading slightly downhill. After the lane bends right, turn right just before Glenkiln Bridge along another lane Ⓑ. Climb gently up the valley of Glen Burn to where the lane bears left a few yards after crossing a smaller burn.

Turn sharp right Ⓒ along a clear track which recrosses the burn

Glenkiln Reservoir

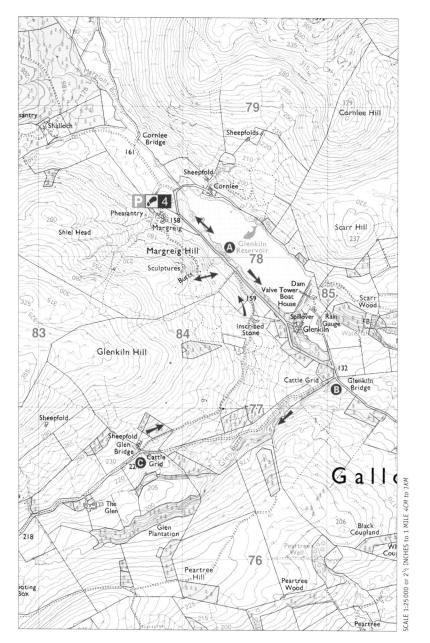

SCALE 1:25 000 or 2½ INCHES to 1 MILE 4CM to 1KM

and later keeps by a wire fence on the left. Go through a metal gate and head gently downhill. As you curve left, fine views open up across the reservoir to Bishop Forest Hill and Cornlee Hill on the far side. After going through a metal gate you reach the site where one of Moore's finest works, *King and Queen*, once stood. They enjoyed a splendid view across the glen.

Go through another metal gate, continue down to the lane and bear left along it to return to the start. ●

Caerlaverock and the Solway Marshes

Start	Castle Wood Car Park
Distance	3½ miles (5.6km)
Height gain	310 feet (95m)
Approximate time	1¾ hours
Parking	Castle Wood Car Park
Ordnance Survey maps	Landranger 84 (Dumfries & Castle Douglas), Explorer 322 (Annandale)

GPS waypoints

☑ NY 019 652
Ⓐ NY 027 651
Ⓑ NY 025 659

A remarkable amount of historic interest and scenic diversity is packed into this short walk on the Solway coast: the extensive ruins of a medieval castle and the earthworks of its predecessor, pleasant woodland, salt marsh, the site of an Iron Age hill fort, plus wonderful views of Criffel on the other side of the Nith Estuary and across the Solway. Be prepared for wet and muddy conditions, with waterlogged paths at times, particularly on the stretch across the marshes.

Caerlaverock, one of the finest of Scottish castles, occupies an important strategic site, guarding one of the main sea routes between England and Scotland. It was built in the 1270s to replace an earlier castle on a less defensible site a few hundred yards to the south and has a triangular shape, described by one of its besiegers in 1300 as 'like a shield... surrounded by an arm of the sea'. The natural defences provided by the woods and marshes were reinforced by a moat and a powerful gatehouse built on the more exposed landward side. Captured by Edward I after a memorable siege in 1300, the castle changed hands several times and suffered much destruction and subsequent rebuilding. As a sign of more settled times, its owner Robert Maxwell, first Earl of Nithsdale, built an elaborate residential block in the 17th century, a fine example

Criffel from Caerlaverock Nature Reserve

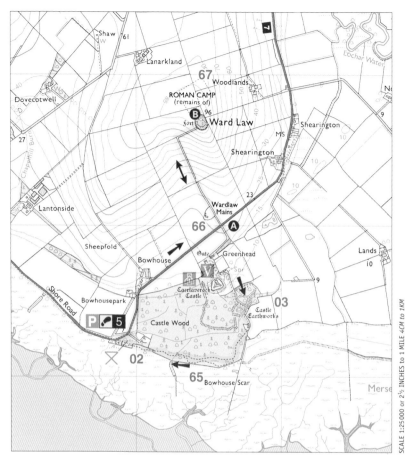

SCALE 1:25 000 or 2½ INCHES to 1 MILE 4CM to 1KM

of Scottish Renaissance architecture, but after its capture by the Covenanters in 1640 the castle fell into ruin.

👣 Exit the car park and turn sharp right along the road for ¾ mile (1.2km) to the sign on the right for Caerlaverock Castle **Ⓐ**. You can turn right for a quick return, but for a brief and worthwhile detour to the Roman fort, turn left along a track and follow the waymarked route uphill, climbing steadily then turning to the right for the final section up to the viewpoint of Ward Law **Ⓑ**.

The earthworks of this Iron Age hill fort was the first of several fortifications in this area. The splendid views that extend over the Solway to the Cumbrian mountains and across the River Nith to Criffel, then inland to the line of the Southern Uplands, indicate the strategic importance of this fort. Retrace your steps to **Ⓐ** then keep ahead along the access road to Caerlaverock Castle. Follow the track past the left of the castle and continue through Castle Woods passing a series of interpretation boards and to the left of the Old Castle Earthworks. It is important that you keep to this road and the track beyond otherwise you will be charged an admission fee. The castle is well worth a visit and has a shop and **tea room**.

The first castle was built in the early

13th century but abandoned after a very short time. Follow the track round right and left bends, pass to the left of two bungalows and continue – now on a footpath – through Castle Wood. There are several points from this path where you can exit onto the marshes of the Caerlaverock Nature Reserve but as this is very wet and boggy wellingtons are advisable. An alternative is to visit the bird hide that can also be accessed from the path. Otherwise keep following the distinct footpath through the wood past a variety of information panels to reach the Castle Woods car park.

Magnificent Caerlaverock Castle

Wigtown

		GPS waypoints
Start	Wigtown	✎ NX 433 552
Distance	4½ miles (7.2km)	Ⓐ NX 436 557
Height gain	280 feet (85m)	Ⓑ NX 438 546
Approximate time	2 hours	Ⓒ NX 425 552
Parking	Wigtown	Ⓓ NX 425 560
Ordnance Survey maps	Explorer 83 (Newton Stewart & Kirkcudbright), Explorer 311 (Wigtown, Whithorn & The Machars)	

This pleasant, easy paced, figure-of-eight walk around Scotland's Book Town can easily be split into two separate shorter walks. There are several reminders of Wigtown's history on the route and from many points you can enjoy superb views across the wide expanses of Wigtown Bay to the outline of the Galloway hills on the horizon.

Once an important royal burgh, port and route centre, with a harbour, castle and monastery, Wigtown is now a sleepy backwater. The huge, triangular open space in the town centre, where the walk begins, is filled with marquees each autumn when the annual book festival is held.

✎ Start at the Mercat Cross where the wide main street divides and take the left-hand street (North Main Street). Pass to the left of the Town Hall and follow the street down to the 19th-century church. Adjoining the church are the ruins of its 18th-century predecessor and in the churchyard are the Martyrs' Graves.

The martyrs were two local women, Margaret McLaughlin and Margaret Wilson, executed in 1685 for supporting the Covenanters, i.e. people who refused to accept the king as head of the Scottish Church. They were tied to a stake in the estuary of the River Bladnoch and drowned by the rising waters as the tide came in. The stones in the churchyard are probably a memorial rather than a grave as executed Covenanters were denied proper burial for fear that they would become recognised as martyrs.

Continue past the church to a small car park and a sign 'Martyrs' Stake', and turn right Ⓐ along a track signposted to Wigtown Harbour. A boardwalk on the left leads to the stake, erected on the supposed site where the two women were drowned. Continue along the footpath from the Martyrs' Stake. Until 1817 this was the site of Wigtown Harbour. You are walking along what was the Wigtown railway line but no trains have run here since 1964. Now a nature reserve the salt marsh on your left is used, during the summer months, for grazing sheep and cattle. In winter the mild climate makes it an attractive winter habitat for many different species of birds from colder parts of the world.

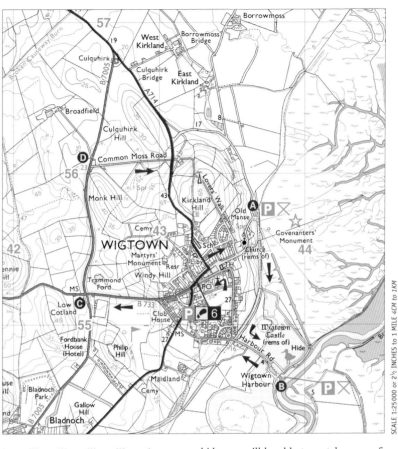

```
0      200    400    600    800 METRES  1
                                        KILOMETRES
                                        MILES
0      200    400    600 YARDS   ½
```

Look out in particular for pink-footed geese.

When the footpath reaches a metal gate it veers left away from the former railway line then continues parallel to it. On your left is the old harbour wall. Follow the path to its junction with a lane opposite the Old Station House and turn left.

Follow this to the harbour **B** then turn left. On the banking in the field across the River Bladnoch is the site of the 13th-century Wigtown Castle. At the end of the harbour continue along a footpath by the riverside to reach the bird hide. Some 15,000 birds spend the winter here and from the hide you will be able to watch many of them including redshank, pintail and lapwing.

Retrace your steps from the hide and when you reach the top of the lane, cross the old railway bridge and turn right along Harbour Road then turn left along South Mains Street passing to the left of the newly renovated town hall, to return to the starting point.

For the second part of the figure-of-eight, continue past the Mercat Cross and take the road ahead, signposted to Kirkcowan. On the hill to the right is the Martyrs' Monument, erected in 1858 in memory of the Wigtown Martyrs. At a crossroads turn right **C**, in the Newton Stewart direction – take care as this is a busy road – and after ½ mile (800m) turn right again **D** on to a straight, enclosed track. The track, later tree-lined, ascends gently to a road.

Cross over the road and at a footpath sign 'Wigtown via Lovers' Walk' keep ahead along a tarmac drive and go through a gate to the left of a bungalow. Now comes a succession of superb views across the bay as you continue gently uphill along a grassy, tree-lined, enclosed track. The track bends right and at a junction of tracks, turn left along another enclosed track. On reaching the edge of the town, continue down a road to a T-junction and then turn right, uphill, to return to the start.

Wigtown Bay

Moffat Well and Gallow Hill

		GPS waypoints
Start	Moffat	🖉 NT 084 054
Distance	4 miles (6.4km)	Ⓐ NT 091 058
Height gain	330 feet (100m)	Ⓑ NT 091 068
Approximate time	2 hours	Ⓒ NT 085 070
Parking	Moffat	
Ordnance Survey maps	Landranger 78 (Nithsdale & Annandale), Explorer 330 (Moffat & St Mary's Loch)	

From the centre of Moffat the route heads gently uphill to Moffat Well, a pleasant spot where Birnock Water tumbles through a narrow, wooded ravine. The return is an attractive and easy descent through the woodlands that clothe Gallow Hill. There are fine views of the encircling hills and across Upper Annandale.

The fountain surmounted by a statue of a ram in the centre of Moffat's unusually wide high street symbolises the town's history as an important wool centre. In the 18th and 19th centuries the town also became a very popular spa and the town hall once housed the baths and pump room. Moffat's attractive location in Upper Annandale and wide assortment of hotels, guest houses, shops, inns and cafés makes the town an excellent touring and walking centre.

Annandale from Gallow Hill

🖉 Start in front of the town hall and with your back to it turn right along High Street. By the war memorial turn left along Well Street, turn right along Well Road and follow it out of town. After just over ½ mile (800m), bear right Ⓐ along Alton Road – a narrow, hedge-lined lane.

At the point where the lane becomes a track, turn left through a metal kissing-gate onto a public footpath to Archbank. Follow the well-waymarked path to the left going through three gates, then veer 45 degrees to the right, to pick up a waymarker. Continue from here to the next wall. Go through a kissing-gate to immediately reach a junction of paths. Ignore the one to the right and keep straight ahead, following waymarkers to pick up a track. Then go through a metal gate and cross a bridge over the Birnock Water. The track now winds uphill

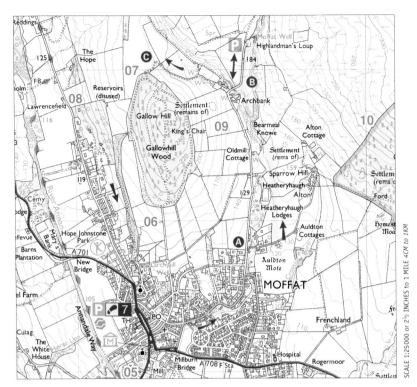

to go through another metal gate on to a lane to the right of a bridge Ⓑ.

Turn right up the lane for ¼ mile (400m) to Moffat Well, reached by turning right through a parking and picnic area and going through a gate. The well was one of a number in the area that helped to make Moffat a popular health resort.

Retrace your steps down the lane to the bridge Ⓑ, cross it and where the lane bends left, turn right through a metal gate and walk along a track. Pass to the left of a line of barns and go through another metal gate. Continue gently uphill, go through a metal gate, keep ahead and the track swings left Ⓒ to continue beside the wall just crossed. On reaching the edge of woodland, turn left through a metal gate and take the path through conifers to meet a track.

Turn right and follow the track downhill through Gallowhill Wood. At

a fork turn right, go through a metal kissing-gate, cross a track and go through another metal kissing-gate. The track bends left and now comes a splendid finale to the walk as you continue down Gallow Hill through delightful broad-leaved woodland. Attractive views over Annandale can be seen through gaps in the trees on the right.

At a fork either track will do – they later rejoin and run parallel – but the right-hand track probably gives the best views. Eventually you join another track by **Beechwood Country House Hotel** and continue downhill. The track becomes a road which bends to the right, passing to the right of St Mary's Church, to the main road. Turn left in front of the church to return to the start. ●

Lochmaben and the Four Lochs

		GPS waypoints
Start	Lochmaben	🥾 NY 080 826
Distance	5½ miles (8.9km)	Ⓐ NY 083 823
Height gain	130 feet (40m)	Ⓑ NY 081 817
Approximate time	2½ hours	Ⓒ NY 084 808
Parking	Lochmaben	Ⓓ NY 088 812
		Ⓔ NY 075 816
Ordnance Survey maps	Landranger 78 (Nithsdale & Annandale), Explorer 322 (Annandale)	Ⓕ NY 073 824
		Ⓖ NY 078 833

The town of Lochmaben in Annandale is surrounded by four lochs – Upper, Mill, Kirk and Castle – and on the south side of Castle Loch, the largest of the four, stand the ruins of a medieval castle. This walk either passes or provides views of all of them and the castle is the main focal point. It is a flat and easy walk that can be done at any time of the year and there are some splendid views across the lochs.

Lochmaben is very much a one street town: at the top end of High Street is the town hall with a statue of Robert the Bruce in front, and at the bottom end is the church.

🥾 Start by the Bruce statue, walk down High Street and in front of the church turn right Ⓐ along Mounsey's Wynd to a T-junction. In front is Castle Hill, the motte of the original 12th-century castle of the Bruces and predecessor of the one on the shores of Castle Loch. Turn left at a Scottish Rights of Way Society public footpath sign and go along a tarmac track. To the right is a golf course and view of Kirk Loch.

Continue along the track, passing to the left of the farm Ⓑ, and go through a metal gate. Continue along the right edge of a field, by a hedge and wire fence on the right, and in the corner

follow the field edge to the left and pass through a metal kissing-gate on to a road. Turn right and at a sign for Lochmaben Castle, turn left Ⓒ along a tarmac drive. After passing a farm entrance, the drive becomes a rough track. Follow it to cross a cattle-grid into woodland to reach the remains of the castle Ⓓ.

Fragmentary though the remains are, Lochmaben Castle has had an interesting and, inevitably for a Border castle occupying an important strategic route between England and Scotland, troubled history.

It belonged to the Bruce family, after they abandoned the earlier castle in the centre of the town, though the first castle on the site was probably built by Edward I in 1298 while on one of his many invasions of Scotland. Lochmaben Castle frequently changed

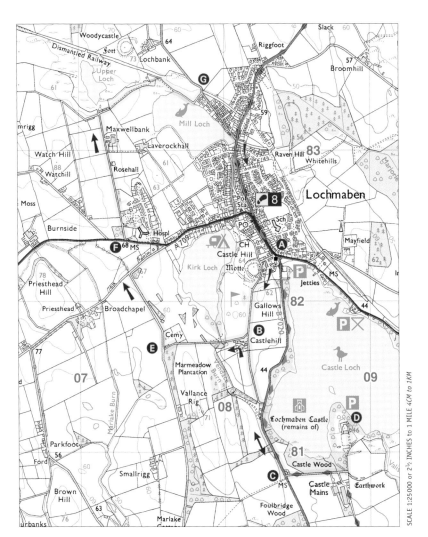

hands and suffered destruction in the almost constant Border warfare, and most of the present remains date from a 14th-century rebuilding. The castle lies in an attractive setting and paths lead down through the trees to the shores of Castle Loch, a nature reserve.

For those wanting a shorter walk and to return to Lochmaben, it is possible to complete a walk around Castle Loch and return to Ⓐ, otherwise retrace your steps to the farm at Castle Hill and at the public footpath sign, turn left through a gate Ⓑ, to continue the route. Walk along a path, enjoying

views across the golf course of Kirk Loch on the right.

Go through another gate, continue, between a conifer wood on the left and a wall bordering a cemetery on the right, to reach a T-junction then turn right on to a lane Ⓔ. Turn right, and at a T-junction turn right again to a main road on the edge of the town and turn sharp left along it. Head uphill past the entrance to the hospital and just past the brow of the hill turn right at a 'No

Through Road' sign ⓕ, and continue along a straight, narrow lane.

Where the lane ends at a T-junction of tracks, there is a view of Upper Loch ahead. Turn right, passing in front of cottages, go through a kissing-gate and keep ahead across grass to pick up and keep beside a hedge on the right. Now come fine views to the right of Mill Loch and the town beyond. Near the end of the field, bear left to a kissing-gate and public footpath sign in the left-hand corner, go through and keep ahead, by a wire fence on the left.

The path curves right and continues through trees that line the shores of Mill Loch. Bear left uphill, now along a track, to a road and turn right ⓖ into Lochmaben. Turn right at a T-junction across the end of the loch, and at a fork, take the left-hand road to return to the start. ●

Lochmaben Castle

Up and Down the Annan

		GPS waypoints
Start	Annan	NY 191 666
Distance	6½ miles (10.5km)	**A** NY 191 667
Height gain	Negligible	**B** NY 187 705
Approximate time	3 hours	**C** NY 186 704
Parking	Everholm Park car park	**D** NY 190 666
Ordnance Survey maps	Explorer 85 (Carlisle & Solway Firth), Explorer 322 (Annandale)	

With an understandable emphasis on hill, lochside, forest and coastal walking in this book, it makes a pleasant change to include a wholly riverside walk, especially such an attractive stretch of the River Annan. The route is easy to follow: upstream along the east bank from Annan to Brydekirk and downstream along the west bank on the Annandale Way, with the two bridges passed before reaching Brydekirk enabling you to shorten the walk at will.

In the 12th century Annan was one of the chief strongholds of the Bruce family and the motte or mound of their former castle is passed near the start of the walk. Later, it became a fishing and shipbuilding centre.

Start from the car park at Everholm Park. Turn right out of the car park and onto the tarmac riverside path **A**. Continue along this by the

The Riverr Annan

banks of the river and passing the castle motte on the right.

Go through a gate and take the tarmac riverside path through the park. To the right is the castle motte. Where the tarmac path ends, pass through a wall gap and keep beside the river up to the road bridge at Brydekirk. En route you pass two footbridges – first a metal one and secondly a suspension bridge.

Cross either bridge and then turn left to curtail the walk and return to Annan.

The well-waymarked undulating path passes through a mixture of woodland and meadows, goes under the Annan bypass, crosses several footbridges over tributary burns and negotiates a number of kissing-gates and stiles. Approaching Brydekirk the river flows between steep wooded banks, a most attractive stretch of the walk.

At the bridge turn left **B** and by the

Brig Inn turn left again along River Street. Where the lane bends right, keep ahead  **C** along the riverside path on the Annandale Way, to follow the other bank back to Annan across the same mixture of woodland and meadow. The only slight complication is that soon after passing the metal footbridge (the second one), continue along a track but look out for where the track bears slightly right. At this point bear left off it to continue along a narrow riverside path.

As you approach Annan there are grand views of the town. Climb a flight of steps by the Annan Bridge **D** then turn left onto the road. Pass the Bluebell Inn and turn left along Battery Street to return to Everholm Park and the start.

Along the River Annan

Fleet Forest and Anwoth Old Kirk

		GPS waypoints
Start	Gatehouse of Fleet	⬛ NX 599 561
Distance	5½ miles (8.9km)	Ⓐ NX 602 563
Height gain	360 feet (110m)	Ⓑ NX 604 554
Approximate time	2½ hours	Ⓒ NX 600 556
Parking	Gatehouse of Fleet	Ⓓ NX 594 559
		Ⓔ NX 586 559
Ordnance Survey maps	Landranger 83 (Newton Stewart & Kirkcudbright), Explorer 312 (Kirkcudbright & Castle Douglas)	Ⓕ NX 582 561
		Ⓖ NX 591 570

This figure-of-eight walk can be divided into two separate shorter walks if desired. The two halves of the walk are completely different. The first half is a flat and easy walk mainly through the attractive woodland of Fleet Forest, and the second half, after initially climbing to a fine viewpoint above the town, is a more hilly route across the heather- and bracken-covered slopes of Boreland Hill.

Pleasantly situated on the Water of Fleet, the main street of Gatehouse of Fleet is dominated by a tall 19th-century clock tower. The Mill on the Fleet, a former cotton mill by the river, is now an exhibition centre featuring the history of the town and local area.

🖊 From the car park turn right along the main street, then turn right through a sandstone arch at the Town Hall following a sign to Garries Park. Walk through a garden, then a metal gate and then along a path which crosses a bridge over a burn and continues into a recreation ground. Turn left along a track by the edge of the recreation ground, pass beside a gate and the track curves right to a T-junction Ⓐ.

Turn right along a tarmac drive, keep ahead to pass beside a gate and continue along what is now a rough

track into woodland. At a crossroads of tracks keep ahead, in the Dalavan direction, and after a few yards you pick up the white, yellow and blue-topped posts of a forest trail. Look out for where a post directs you to turn right on to a winding path.

Cross a footbridge over a burn, keep ahead at the next post, pass a white and yellow-topped post and head up to a T-junction of paths. Turn right and the path emerges on to a tarmac drive Ⓑ.

Turn right and take the first track on the left, signposted 'Cricket Ground'. The track curves left, heads gently downhill and bears right to cross a burn. Follow the track to the left and a few yards before it crosses another burn and bends right, turn sharp right on to a path Ⓒ. After crossing a burn the path turns left to keep beside it. Cross a track and keep ahead to meet

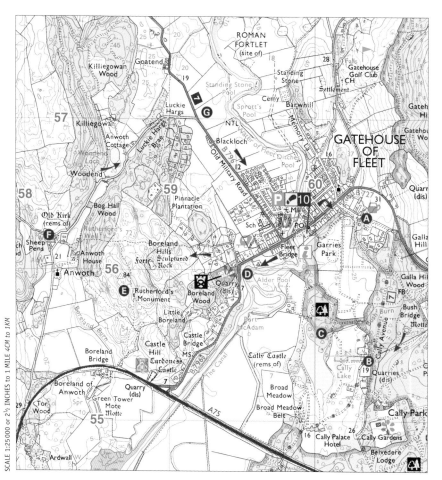

SCALE 1:25000 or 2½ INCHES to 1 MILE 4CM to 1KM

a track at a U-bend just in front of the recreation ground. Take the left-hand track to the river and cross a footbridge over a burn. Keep ahead, go through a gate and walk across a picnic area to return to the car park.

For the second part of the figure-of-eight, turn left out of the car park and cross the bridge over the Water of Fleet. Where the road bears left, turn right **D** through a kissing-gate, at a National Trust for Scotland sign 'Venniehill'. For a short detour, follow a winding grassy path uphill – plenty of yellow waymarks – to a toposcope and a viewpoint over the town, Fleet Forest and the surrounding hills.

Descend to the road **D** and turn

left along a lane. The lane curves left uphill and by a cattle-grid, bear slightly left to go through a metal gate at a public footpath sign. Walk along a narrow path, between a wall on the right and trees on the left, go through a gate and climb first a stone stile and immediately after another stile. Turn right, continue uphill across a grassy slope dotted with trees and then follow a winding path – looking out for yellow waymarks – across the gorse, heather and bracken of Boreland Hill.

Follow the path by a wall then turn right, through a gap, to reach a wooden

0   200   400   600   800 METRES   1
━━━━━━━━━━━━━━━━━━━━━━━━━━━━━━━━━━━━   KILOMETRES
0   200   400   600 YARDS   ½   MILES

stile. Cross this and continue on the well-waymarked path heading towards three prominent landmarks on the skyline ahead. The tall one on the left is the Rutherford Monument. To the right is the Millenium Monument and a triangulation pillar.

First make your way up to the monument **E**, a superb viewpoint overlooking the Fleet Estuary and Wigtown Bay. It was erected in 1842 in memory of Samuel Rutherford, a 17th-century scholar, religious teacher and minister at nearby Anwoth church.

Turn right at the Rutherford Monument and head across to the next one following the waymarks. This was erected by local people to mark the new millenium and lists all the ministers of Girthorn and Anwoth churches from the Reformation. Cross from here to the triangulation pillar, then continue in the same direction following the waymarkers. Go down a dip and up again then descend downhill through bracken to the edge of a wood. Go past the remains of a metal gate and into the woods ignoring a turning on the right indicated by an old yellow marker post.

Follow the path downhill through this attractive woodland, then, at the bottom, go through a metal gate into a field. Follow the path from here to the corner of the churchyard then go through a metal gate and along a path beside the churchyard wall. The path ends at a junction with a lane. Turn right onto this **F**.

The atmospheric ruins of the Old Kirk date from the 17th century and the church remained in use until the early 19th century when it was replaced by the new church about ¼ mile (400m) to the south. The tower of the new church will have been clearly seen from the triangulation pillar.

Turn right along the lane in front of the Old Kirk and follow it for nearly one mile (1.6km) to a T-junction **G**. Turn right along a road back into Gatehouse of Fleet and at a T-junction turn left over Fleet Bridge to return to the start. ●

The view from Boreland Hill

Wanlockhead and Lowther Hill

		GPS waypoints
Start	Wanlockhead	☞ NS 873 129
Distance	4½ miles (7.2km)	Ⓐ NS 875 128
Height gain	1,015 feet (310m)	Ⓑ NS 883 114
Approximate time	2½ hours	Ⓒ NS 887 107
Parking	Museum of Lead Mining car park at Wanlockhead	Ⓓ NS 889 103
Ordnance Survey maps	Landrangers 71 (Lanark & Upper Nithsdale) and 78 (Nithsdale & Annandale), Explorer 329 (Lowther Hills, Sanquhar & Leadhills)	

The route follows a section of the Southern Upland Way southwards from the village of Wanlockhead to the summit of Lowther Hill (2,378ft/725m), easily distinguished by the 'golf ball' of the radar station there. The climb is a continuous and steady one across the grassy slopes of the hill, made considerably easier by the starting point being at over 1,500ft (457m). On both the ascent and descent there are wide and extensive views over the surrounding hills. It is advisable not to attempt this walk in misty weather.

The old lead mining village of Wanlockhead, 1,531ft (466m) high, is Scotland's highest village, and cradled by the bare and lonely Lowther Hills, it is both uniquely interesting and highly atmospheric. Lead has been mined in the area since the 13th century but mining activity was at its height in the 18th and 19th centuries and the last mines closed in the 1950s. The whole place is an outdoor living museum and it is worthwhile following a trail from the visitor centre that takes you down a mine and into miners' cottages, past a spoil heap, smelt mills and a beam engine, enabling you to get some idea of what life was like in this isolated community in the heyday of the mines.

☞ Start the walk by climbing the flight of steps that lead off from the end of the museum car park. Head

Wanlockhead

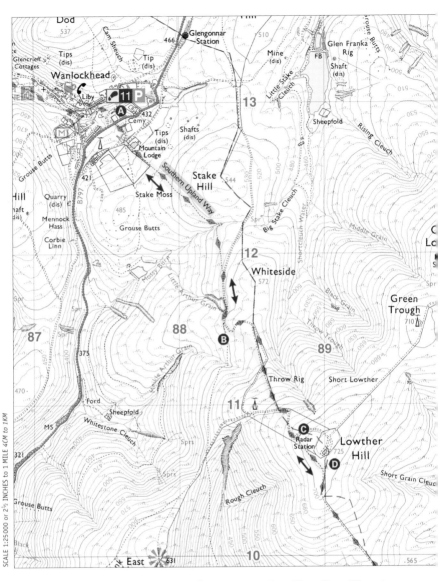

across the grass, cross a stony track and continue along a grassy track to a road **Ⓐ**.

Cross over the road and follow the Southern Upland Way uphill on a track that passes some new houses.

Continue uphill, by a wire fence on the right, and where the fence ends, follow the clear track ahead across the heathery hillside.

Turn right to cross a footbridge over a burn and continue up to the

road which winds up to the Radar Station, now used by NATS (National Air Traffic Services). This road is crossed several times as, fortunately, the Southern Upland Way takes a more direct route.

Turn right along the road but at a sharp left-hand bend **Ⓑ**, continue along the path which can clearly be seen ahead, the route marked with regular Southern Upland Way posts. Recross the road, continue uphill, by a wire fence on the left, cross the road on two more occasions and eventually join it again just to the right of the radar station.

Turn right along the road as far as a left-hand bend where you turn right and head across grass to climb a stile on the right in front of the radar station 'golf ball'. Turn left and continue in the same direction to reach a stile in a wire fence just below the summit . There are superb all-round views from here across the rolling, empty Lowther Hills, and looking down the length of Nithsdale the Solway Firth can be seen in the distance.

From here retrace your steps downhill back to the start. The Museum of Lead Mining visitor centre has a **café**. ●

The old school at Wanlockhead

Water of Luce and Kilhern

		GPS waypoints
Start	New Luce	
Distance	5½ miles (8.9km)	NX 174 647
Height gain	345 feet (105m)	Ⓐ NX 174 626
Approximate time	2½ hours	Ⓑ NX 200 638
Parking	Roadside parking in New Luce	Ⓒ NX 191 650
Ordnance Survey maps	Landranger 82 (Stranraer & Glenluce), Explorer 310 (Glenluce & Kirkcowan)	

About half the walk is along quiet roads and narrow lanes in the lush valley of the Water of Luce. The remainder follows a section of the Southern Upland Way across expanses of open, heathery moorland, more reminiscent perhaps of parts of the Pennines than the rest of Galloway. On the descent from the prehistoric burial chamber at Kilhern back into the valley, the views are particularly memorable.

The quiet village of New Luce is attractively situated where the Main Water of Luce and the Cross Water of Luce unite to form the Water of Luce.

🥾 Start by the Southern Upland Way information shelter at the T-junction in the village centre and walk southwards, in the Glenluce direction. Cross a bridge over the Cross

Moorland near New Luce

Water of Luce, pass to the right of the church and continue along the road for 1¼ miles (2km). There are very pleasant views to the right across the valley.

At a Southern Upland Way sign opposite a farm entrance on the right Ⓐ, turn left over a ladder-stile and take an uphill track. On reaching three metal gates, climb a stile beside the middle one of the three and walk along the left edge of a field, by a wall on the left, to climb another ladder-stile.

Ahead are three tracks: continue along the middle one which heads in a straight line across open moorland for 1¾ miles (2.8km). Climb a ladder-stile, keep ahead and on approaching the ruined farm at Kilhern, follow the direction of a Southern Upland Way

post to the left **B**.

Keep by a wall on the right, go over a stile and at another waymarked post, turn left to continue across the moorland. Keep on this track to reach a wall with an open gate. A sign points right from here to the 'Caves of Kilhern 200 metres,' a Neolithic burial chamber probably constructed around 4000 – 5000 years ago. When the track turns right through a gate keep ahead through another metal gate and follow the waymarkers along the edge

of a wall, passing a conifer plantation, and after the wall ends continue to a Southern Upland Way post.

Turn left along a track down to a lane and turn left **C** along this narrow lane, heading gently downhill to the church at New Luce. At a T-junction by the church, turn right to return to the start, passing the **Kenmuir Arms Hotel**. ●

Rascarrel Bay and Balcary Point

Start	Balcary Bay, at end of minor road from Auchencairn
Distance	5 miles (8km)
Height gain	310 feet (95m)
Approximate time	2½ hours
Parking	Balcary Bay
Ordnance Survey maps	Landranger 84 (Dumfries & Castle Douglas), Explorer 313 (Dumfries & Dalbeattie)

GPS waypoints

- ✍ NX 821 494
- Ⓐ NX 801 488
- Ⓑ NX 799 482
- Ⓒ NX 826 495

From Balcary Bay the first part of the route heads inland – across fields, beside an attractive loch and through a conifer plantation – to rejoin the coast at Rascarrel Bay. The rest of the walk follows the coast, initially along the edge of a stony beach, later climbing on to low cliffs and finally rounding the steep and dramatic headland of Balcary Point, the scenic highlight of the walk. On this last stretch comes a succession of spectacular views over Auchencairn Bay and across the Solway Firth to the Cumbrian mountains.

✍ From the car park take the tarmac track signposted 'Right of Way to Loch Mackie and Rascarrel Bay'. Where the main track bears left, keep ahead – at a footpath sign – along a rough track, passing to the right of a house.

Go through a metal gate, keep along the track by a wall on the left, but after going through a kissing-gate the route continues along a narrow path beside Loch Mackie. Go through the second of two kissing-gates at the Loch signposted for Balcary. Cross a footbridge, ignore a faint path to the right, then at a fork where a faint path leads off to the left, turn right to continue along the edge of woodland to a junction with a track. Turn left

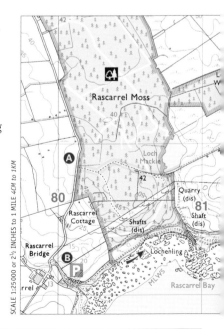

SCALE 1:25000 or 2½ INCHES to 1 MILE 4CM to 1KM

Balcary Bay

and continue along the track to reach a lane **Ⓐ**.

Turn left and after ½ mile (800m), turn left again **Ⓑ**, at a sign 'Rascarrel Bay Coastal Path', along a hedge- and tree-lined track. The track continues beside the stony shore of Rascarrel Bay and after passing in front of some cottages, narrows to a path.

Later, the path climbs on to low cliffs and continues to a metal kissing-gate. Go through and now comes a series of spectacular and ever-changing views, across the Solway and later over Auchencairn Bay to Hestan Island and the coast beyond, as the path rounds the rocky headland of Balcary Point. *On this part of the walk there are some steep climbs and there are notices warning you to take care as at times the path comes very close to the cliff edge.*

After rounding the point, continue through attractive woodland to a kissing-gate **Ⓒ**. Go through, keep along the right edge of a field – variously trees, wall and a wire fence on the right – pass to the left of a house and bear right in the field corner to go through another kissing-gate. Walk along an enclosed track to return to the start. ●

Screel Hill

		GPS waypoints
Start	New Forestry Commission's Screel Wood car park, about 200 yds along minor road, left off A711, 2 miles (3.2km) north of Auchencairn	🥾 NX 800 546 Ⓐ NX 793 546 Ⓑ NX 779 553 Ⓒ NX 782 550
Distance	3½ miles (5.6km)	
Height gain	1,085 feet (330m)	
Approximate time	2½ hours	
Parking	Screel Wood	
Ordnance Survey maps	Landranger 84 (Dumfries & Castle Douglas), Explorer 312 (Kirkcudbright & Castle Douglas)	

Screel Hill rises to the north of the village of Auchencairn and, despite its modest height of 1,126ft (344m), the summit provides grand, extensive and uninterrupted views over the Galloway hills and along the Solway coast. The route follows a waymarked Forestry Commission trail and the climb is a steady one, though near the top the going becomes steeper and rockier. The descent is very easy and straightforward. Do not attempt this walk in bad weather and mist conditions unless experienced in such conditions and able to navigate by using a compass.

🥾 Pass beside the gate at the end of the car park, in the 'Screel Hill Walk' direction, and follow a winding, steadily ascending track through conifers.

At a track intersection, keep ahead uphill on a narrower, rougher path, bisecting the crossing track, following a red waymarker. The path emerges on to a track Ⓐ, cross it and continue uphill, passing to the right of a bench from which there is a fine view over the Solway. Head up through the trees and after crossing a footbridge, turn left to reach a reassuring waymark. Eventually you emerge from the forest into an open area of bracken and heather.

Continue more steeply now along a rocky path, keeping to the left of a line of crags. Bengairn is the wooded hill over to the left and the summit of Screel Hill can be seen ahead. Make your way through the rocks – the path becomes indistinct at this point and you have to cross some marshy ground – on to the ridge and follow it as it curves gradually to the left to reach the summit cairn Ⓑ. There are fine views from here: in one direction along the Solway coast and over the water to the line of the Cumbrian fells on the horizon; in the other direction across to the Galloway hills. Below, Castle Douglas can clearly be seen beside Carlingwark Loch.

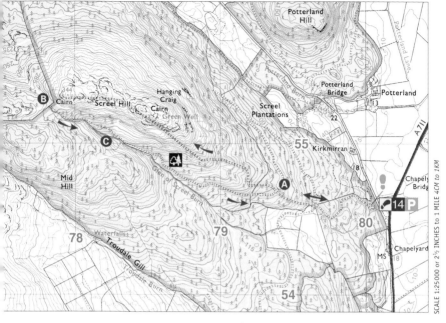

SCALE 1:25000 or 2½ INCHES to 1 MILE 4CM to 1KM

At the cairn bear left, in the direction of Bengairn, descending to a col, and here turn sharply left to take a steeply descending, winding path.

Continue along the edge of the forest, by a wall on the right, but look out for an obvious path on the left through the conifers. Head gently

downhill to emerge on to a track **C**.

Continue downhill on the track until you reach the track junction **A**. Here turn right and retrace your steps down to the start.

Screel Hill

Water of Ken and Garroch Glen

		GPS waypoints	
Start	St John's Town of Dalry		NX 619 812
Distance	4½ miles (7.2km)	**Ⓐ**	NX 611 804
Height gain	510 feet (155m)	**Ⓑ**	NX 606 806
Approximate time	2½ hours	**Ⓒ**	NX 597 820
Parking	Roadside parking in centre of St John's Town of Dalry	**Ⓓ**	NX 613 817
Ordnance Survey maps	Landranger 77 (Dalmellington & New Galloway), Explorer 318 (Galloway Forest Park North)		

The walk begins by following the Water of Ken downstream and continues along a quiet and pleasant lane through Garroch Glen. Then follows an easy and gentle climb over Waterside Hill that provides you with a series of outstandingly attractive views over the Ken valley and St John's Town of Dalry as you descend back to the start. Waterproof boots are advisable as part of the route is boggy.

St John's Town of Dalry – Dalry for short – beautifully situated above the Water of Ken, is only a village in size but it has the feel and appearance of a small town. The close proximity of the

St John's Town of Dalry

town hall, the motte of a 12th-century castle, and church help to create this impression. The church, seen prominently on the latter stages of the walk, was built in 1831 and beside it is the ruined Gordon Aisle of its medieval predecessor, former burial place of the

Gordons of nearby Lochinvar.

✏️ The walk starts by the fountain in the town centre. Take the track to the right of the town hall, at a Southern Upland Way fingerpost, and continue along a path which descends to the Water of Ken. The castle motte is to the right and the church to the left.

Cross the suspension footbridge over the river, turn left and follow a rough footpath down the western bank of the Water of Ken, dodging between gorse bushes (if the river is high it is easier to go through the first gate on the right into a field and walk down the edge of it). Further down, step over the fence where it is ruined into the field and cross a footbridge over a small stream. Veer left through a pedestrian gate and continue ahead along the top of a grassy levee, which eventually bends right to a gate onto the A762 **Ⓐ**.

Turn left, cross the first of two bridges, and then go immediately right on a rather overgrown footpath signed Glenlee. Follow it along another levee, continuing ahead when the embankment bends left then turning left through a gate to walk along the right side of a ditch. Cross two footbridges

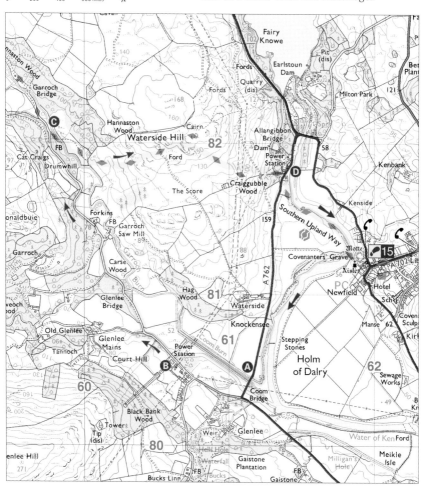

St John's Town of Dalry from Waterside Hill

and climb up to a gate **B** beside Glenlee Hydroelectric Power Station, built in 1934. Turn right and follow a quiet lane through Garroch Glen. After 1½ miles (2.4km) turn right **C**, at a Southern Upland Way fingerpost, along a narrow path through trees.

The path bears right beside Garroch Burn, turns left to cross a footbridge over it and turns right to keep parallel to a fence on the right. This part is waterlogged with some sections of boardwalk that are too short to avoid all the mud. Under some trees, go through a gate in a stone wall and skirt the last boggy area. Now follow a series of waymarked posts marking a grassy path that weaves up to the left and climbs over rocky Waterside Hill. At the top of the hill comes the first of a series of superb views over the Ken valley.

Descend gently and, towards the bottom, approach a wall on the right. Keep outside it and go through a gate in the lower corner of the open grazing. Follow an enclosed path down to a road – to the left is Earlstoun water power station. Cross the road diagonally to the right **D**. Follow the Southern Upland Way along the bank until the suspension bridge is reached and retrace your steps to the start. ●

Devil's Beef Tub

		GPS waypoints
Start	Devil's Beef Tub, at Covenanters' Monument on east side of A701, about 5 miles (8km) north of Moffat	✏ NT 062 125 Ⓐ NT 055 127 Ⓑ NT 055 138 Ⓒ NT 058 132 Ⓓ NT 067 132
Distance	5½ miles (8.9km)	
Height gain	740 feet (255m)	
Approximate time	3 hours	
Parking	Lay-by at Covenanters' Memorial, others nearby	
Ordnance Survey maps	Landranger 78 (Nithsdale & Annandale), Explorer 330 (Moffat & St Mary's Loch)	

The Devil's Beef Tub, a large, deep, natural depression at the head of Annandale, acquired its name from its earlier reputation as a place where the Border reivers (gangs of marauders and thieves) used to hide their stolen cattle. It can easily be viewed from the A701 but it is seen to much greater effect on this walk which encircles three sides of it and climbs Annanhead Hill and Great Hill, both dramatic vantage points overlooking it. Along the crest of the hills, the route follows the northernmost part of the Annandale Way, a long distance walk from river source to sea. Expect some boggy walking in places across rough, grassy moorland.

Looking across the Devil's Beef Tub to Great Hill

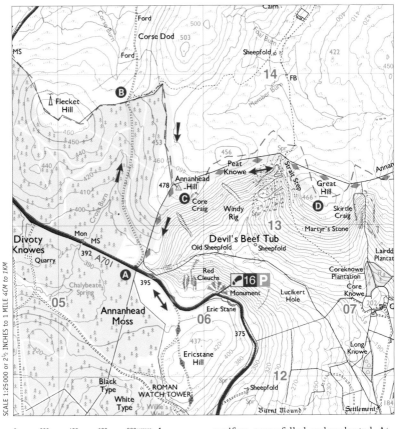

At the side of the road a gate gives access to the Covenanters' Monument and immediately provides a glorious view over the Devil's Beef Tub. The monument is one of many scattered throughout Dumfries and Galloway to the Covenanters of the 17th century, persecuted and executed for refusing to accept the king as head of the Scottish Church.

Facing the Devil's Beef Tub, turn left along the road – there is a verge – and after ½ mile (800m) turn right **A** through a gate by an Annandale Way signpost. The Way soon goes right, out of the forest by a gate – this is the return route. Stay on the track, which bears left and continues gently uphill between

conifers, some felled and replanted. At the top go through a gate (or climb over if it is locked) and emerge from the trees. From here there is a fine view over the rolling Tweedsmuir Hills and in the depression ahead is the source of the River Tweed. The Devil's Beef Tub itself is the source of the Annan.

Turn right **B** and keep alongside a wire fence bordering the forest on the right, heading steadily uphill across rough, tussocky grass. Follow the fence where it turns sharp right, initially still keeping along the forest edge, but later the fence bears slightly left away from it. The moorland here is badly drained and likely to be waterlogged and muddy. Continue steadily uphill towards the triangulation pillar seen ahead. Go through a gate a few yards in from a fence corner to reach it on the summit of Annanhead Hill (1,569ft/478m) . A nearby bench offers a fine and extensive view over the forested slopes of the Southern Uplands.

Turn left, now back on the Annandale Way, with a wire fence and ruined wall on the left and superb views of the Devil's Beef Tub to the right. Descend into the tight, rocky col between Annanhead Hill and Great Hill. Cross the col with care then bear slightly right of the fence line to climb to the summit of Great Hill (1,531ft/466m) . Here are even more spectacular views over the encircling hills, with the Devil's Beef Tub immediately below.

From here retrace your steps back to Annanhead Hill then bear left downhill with the fence on your right to follow the Annandale Way back to the road, there turning left to return to the start. ●

Along the route to Great Hill from Annandale Hill

Loch Trool

Start	Bridge over the River Trool 1½ miles (2.4km) east of Glen Trool Visitor Centre at Stroan Bridge	**GPS waypoints** ✐ NX 397 791 Ⓐ NX 430 799 Ⓑ NX 415 803 Ⓒ NX 401 798
Distance	5½ miles (8.9km)	
Height gain	475 feet (145m)	
Approximate time	3 hours	
Parking	There is space for several cars on a hard standing area beside the bridge	
Ordnance Survey maps	Landranger 77 (Dalmellington & New Galloway), Explorer 319 (Galloway Forest Park South)	

This is arguably the finest short walk in Dumfries and Galloway. For a modest distance and moderate effort, you enjoy the most outstanding views across Loch Trool to the surrounding peaks from many different angles as you circuit the loch. The route is well-waymarked and easy to follow but there is likely to be some muddy and rough stretches. It is worth choosing a fine day and taking your time over this walk.

The area around Loch Trool is associated with some of the most momentous events in Scottish history. A short distance (and signposted) from the start is the Martyr's Tomb, marking the place where six Covenanters were executed in 1685 for refusing to accept Charles II as head of the Church of Scotland. The route later passes the site of a battle between the Scots and English in 1307, and the Bruce Stone which commemorates Robert the Bruce's victory in that battle. *The Loch Trool Loop runs through a working forest; if any part of the route is closed for felling operations, follow the Forestry Commission diversion signs.*

✐ Start at the bridge over the Water of Trool and bear right, following for the first half of the walk both Southern Upland Way marker

posts and green-topped 'Loch Trool Trail' posts. Turn left to cross a footbridge over Caldons Burn, continue along a path beside it to reach a tarmac drive. Turn left, then turn left again and continue along the tarmac drive which curves to the right. Turn left along a track, following the waymarks, cross a burn and shortly bear right along a path through woodland. The path curves uphill to a kissing-gate. Go through to enter conifer plantations.

The next part of the walk is particularly attractive as you follow a switchback route – with some quite steep climbs at times – through woodland above Loch Trool. The views across the water to the hills on the north side, including a striking view of Merrick at one point, are magnificent.

Near the end of the loch the path passes the location of the Battle of Glentrool in 1307 where the Scots, under Robert the Bruce, ambushed an English army and defeated it by rolling boulders down the steep slopes on to the English cavalry.

Eventually the path descends to Glenhead Burn . Cross the footbridge ahead, here leaving the Southern Upland Way, turn left alongside the tree-lined burn and bear right away from it, following green-topped posts, to a track. Turn left and now comes another attractive part of the walk as you proceed through delightful deciduous woodland. After crossing Gairland Burn the track ascends to a gate. Go through, keep ahead to cross a bridge over Buchan Burn and follow the track uphill. Just after a right bend, turn left along an uphill path to Bruce's Stone **B**, a fine viewpoint overlooking Loch Trool and the scene of the king's victory in 1307.

Turn right to rejoin the track by a

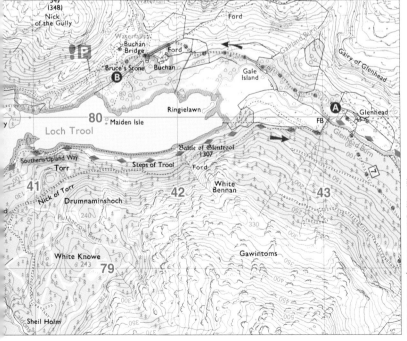

car park and turn left along a lane, passing through a second car park. Continue along the lane for one mile (1.6km) and look out for where a green-topped post directs you to turn left into conifer woodland **Ⓒ**.

Cross a footbridge over a burn and then follow a winding and undulating path back through the trees to the start. ●

Loch Trool

St Ninian's Cave and Burrow Head

		GPS waypoints
Start	Kidsdale car park. Take A746 south-west from Whithorn, turn left on to A747 and turn right along lane signposted to Kidsdale car park	✎ NX 431 366 Ⓐ NX 432 364 Ⓑ NX 426 358 Ⓒ NX 421 360 Ⓓ NX 458 340
Distance	7½ miles (12.1km). Shorter version 2 miles (3.2km)	
Height gain	475ft (145m). Shorter version 150ft (45m)	
Approximate time	3½ hours (1 hour for shorter walk)	
Parking	Kidsdale	
Ordnance Survey maps	Landranger 83 (Newton Stewart & Kirkcudbright), Explorer 311 (Wigtown, Whithorn & The Machars)	

A short walk through the beautiful, wooded Physgill Glen brings you to the coast by St Ninian's Cave. After visiting this historic site, associated with the beginnings of Scottish Christianity, the shorter version of the walk returns directly to the start, but the full walk heads eastwards across the cliffs to the prominent headland of Burrow Head. The coastal scenery between St Ninian's Cave and Burrow Head is superb. Be prepared for thickets of gorse between Ⓑ and Ⓓ as, in summer, T-shirts and shorts will not give adequate protection.

✎ Exit the car park following the signs to St Ninian's Cave. Follow a well-surfaced footpath between two wire fences to go through a gate and cross a lane to a signpost to St Ninian's Cave Ⓐ and continue along a track. This straight track – it later narrows to a path – leads through the steep-sided, wooded Physgill Glen, keeping to the right of a burn. In late spring the ground is carpeted with bluebells. After passing through a gate, the path

St Ninian's Cave

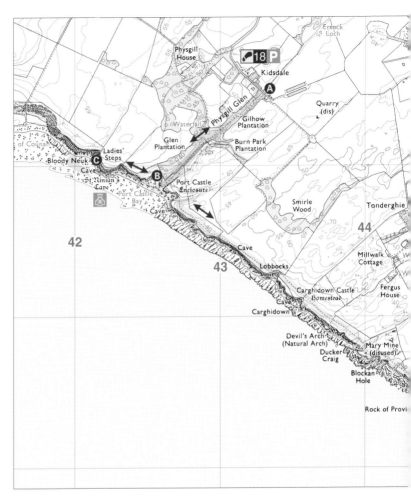

becomes less wooded and then emerges on to a stony beach **B**.

Turn right to St Ninian's Cave **C**. St Ninian is alleged to have founded the first church in Scotland at nearby Whithorn in AD397; the legendary *Candida Casa* or White House. In the following centuries a great monastery was established on the site and the shrine of St Ninian became a major centre of pilgrimage. Several Scottish kings and queens made the journey to Whithorn, the last being Mary Queen of Scots in 1567. The monastery was also

the cathedral of the medieval bishops of Galloway. According to legend, St Ninian used this cave as a retreat and therefore it also attracted the attention of the pilgrims, along with the 12th-century St Ninian's Chapel a few miles away at Isle of Whithorn.

Return to the start of the path through Physgill Glen **B**.

For the shorter walk, turn left here and retrace your steps to the car park.

For the full walk, carry on to the far end of the beach and take the path ahead that climbs steeply past a coastal footpath fingerpost on to the cliff top. At the next fingerpost go through a kissing-gate and continue along the

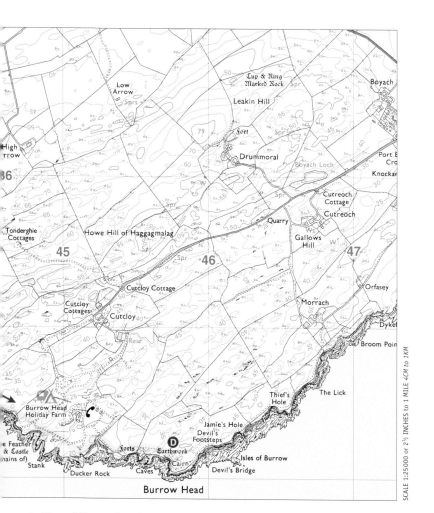

The following labels appear on the map:

Low Arrow, Cup & Ring Marked Rock, Boyach, Spr, Leakin Hill, High rrow, Fort, 79, 70, Drummoral, Spr, 60, 55, Boyach Loch, Port E Cro, Knockar, 36, 65, 70, 65, W, Cutreoch Cottage, Cutreoch, Tonderghie Cottages, 45, Howe Hill of Haggagmalag, Spr, 46, Spr, Quarry, W, Gallows Hill, W, 47, Orfasey, 50, Cutcloy Cottage, 40, Morrach, Cutcloy Cottages, Cutcloy, 40, Dyke, Resr, Broom Poin, 35, 30, 25, Burrow Head Holiday Farm, Thief's Hole, The Lick, e Feather & Castle ains of), Jamie's Hole, Devil's Footsteps, Stank, Forts, Earthwork, 20, Caves, Cairn, Isles of Burrow, Ducker Rock, Devil's Bridge

Burrow Head

SCALE 1:25000 or 2½ INCHES to 1 MILE 4CM to 1KM

path. There follows a fine, bracing and spectacular walk along the cliffs with a couple of kissing-gates to go through. *There are sections with steep drops so proceed with great care.* After passing through a kissing-gate the route heads across more open, grassy expanses – an undulating route with a few burns to ford – to a stone stile. Climb it and continue to a kissing-gate, beyond which is a holiday park.

Go through the gate and follow the coast along the edge of the park. Exit via a kissing-gate beside a public footpath sign and head up to the cairn on Burrow Head **D** where you can enjoy the grand and extensive views.

From here retrace your steps back to the start. ●

Cliffs near St Ninian's Cave

Manquhill Hill

Start	Stroanpatrick, on B729, 2 miles (3.2km) north-east of junction with B7000 and ¾ mile (1.2km) east of bridge over Water of Ken
Distance	6¾ miles (10.6km)
Height gain	900 feet (275m)
Approximate time	3½ hours
Parking	On verge in front of tin hut at Stroanpatrick
Ordnance Survey maps	Landranger 77 (Dalmellington & New Galloway), Explorer 328 (Sanquhar & New Cumnock)

GPS waypoints

⬛ NX 643 917
Ⓐ NX 642 917
Ⓑ NX 657 937
Ⓒ NX 667 955
Ⓓ NX 666 941

This is a walk of wide and sweeping vistas across an austere, largely empty but undeniably beautiful landscape of rolling hills, typical of the Southern Uplands. It follows a lonely stretch of the Southern Upland Way from the tiny hamlet of Stroanpatrick over the slopes of Manquhill Hill, an easy ascent. The return loops around the eastern flank of Manquhill Hill to join the outward route. A shorter option is to treat this as a there-and-back walk to Manquhill Hill. It is advisable not to attempt this walk in misty weather.

🥾 Facing the tin hut, turn right along the road and at a Southern Upland Way fingerpost turn right on to a track Ⓐ. In front of the gate to Stroanpatrick Farm, bear left to ford a burn then slip under a single strand electric fence. Keep ahead to a Southern Upland Way post and turn right to follow a reasonably clear path – likely to be muddy in places – keeping roughly parallel to a wall on the right.

The path climbs gently, there are several burns to ford, some stiles to climb and regular marker posts to show the way. All around are superb views: behind, the Rhinns of Kells and in front, the Carsphairn range.

After climbing a ladder-stile the wall on the right ends and in a short distance the path reaches a forest road Ⓑ where you turn left. Soon turn right at a junction onto a newer forest road, and then turn left at a gap in the trees to continue on the Southern Upland Way. The path, clearer now and better drained, continues uphill through a conifer plantation. Later it climbs more steeply over the left shoulder of Manquhill Hill (1,382ft/421m) and then descends gently into the col between Manquhill Hill and Benbrack which looms ahead. Away to the left are extensive conifer plantations.

On meeting a broad stony track Ⓒ

0	200	400	600	800 METRES	**1**	
						KILOMETRES
						MILES
0	200	400	600 YARDS	½		

turn sharp right on to it. The track curves right and heads gently downhill. Keep left where the track forks, then at a T-junction **D** keep right and follow the plantation track around to the junction encountered earlier in the walk at **B**. Here turn left and retrace the outbound route back to the start. ●

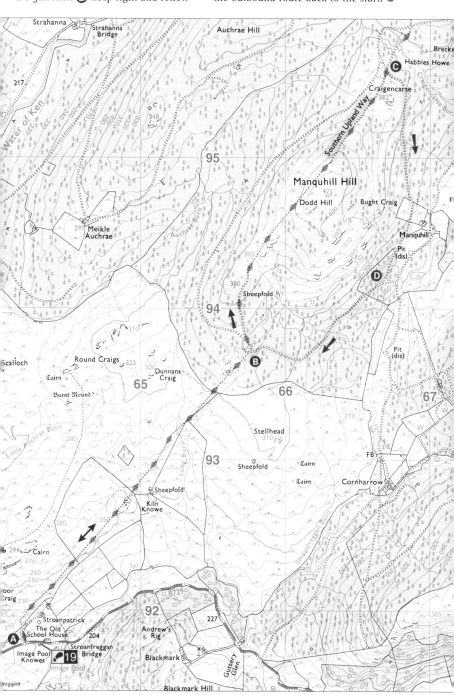

Portpatrick and Killantringan Fell

		GPS waypoints	
Start	Portpatrick		NW 998 542
Distance	8 miles (12.9km)	**A**	NW 994 544
Height gain	1,380 feet (420m)	**B**	NW 982 566
Approximate time	4 hours	**C**	NW 993 571
Parking	Portpatrick	**D**	NW 995 568
Ordnance Survey maps	Landranger 82 (Stranraer & Glenluce), Explorer 309 (Stranraer & The Rhins)		

The starting point of the walk is also the starting point for the 212-mile (340km) Southern Upland Way. This route follows the first four miles (6.4km) of the Southern Upland Way and then retraces steps; a highly enjoyable walk that provides spectacular cliff scenery and fine views along the coast. There are several climbs up and down cliffs and the short ascent of Killantringan Fell is across rough ground.

Situated amidst beautiful cliff scenery and sandy beaches and with cottages grouped around a small fishing harbour, it is not surprising that Portpatrick has developed into a popular though quiet resort. But for its exposed position on the west coast of Galloway, it might have become a major port – it is the nearest point on the British mainland to Ireland – but it lost out to Stranraer at the head of the sheltered Loch Ryan. Portpatrick gets its name from St Patrick who is alleged to have crossed over from Ireland in one stride. Just behind the harbour are the ruins of a 17th-century church with a round tower.

The walk begins at the harbour. Facing the sea, turn right along the road and follow the harbour round to the left to the shelter at the base of the cliffs that marks the official start of the Southern Upland Way.

From here climb the zigzag steps on to the cliff top, pass to the left of a British Telecom Radio Station and turn right up steps to a lane **A**. Turn left – there is a golf course on the right – and the lane becomes first a rough track and then narrows to a cliff-top path. Descend a steep path to a bay, cross a stony beach, climb steps on the other side and turn left at a Southern Upland Way post. Shortly walk across another stony beach where there is a footbridge over a burn.

Pass through a gap in the cliffs on the right, looking out for the waymarked posts, and then ascend two series of steps. *These are rough, deep and difficult in places, but there is a chain provided for support.*

At the top of the steps turn left over a stile and continue along the smooth,

grassy cliffs. Soon the lighthouse on Black Head is seen ahead and you follow a well-waymarked, undulating route towards it, negotiating two kissing-gates on the way.

Pass to the right of the lighthouse to reach a tarmac lane **B** and turn right along it. To the left are lovely views along the length of Killantringan Bay.

Just after the lane bends left by Killantringan Cottage, turn right **C** at the first passing place to go through a gate and head up the rough, grassy slopes (likely to be muddy and boggy near the bottom) of Killantringan Fell. Carefully pick your way between the rocks and gorse to reach the triangulation pillar on the summit **D**. Although only 497ft (151m) high, this is a grand viewpoint, both along the coast in either direction and over inland Galloway.

Retrace your steps to the start, *taking particular care on the descent of the deep steps to Maidenhead Bay. Approaching Portpatrick you enjoy superb views over the harbour.* ●

Portpatrick harbour

Mabie Forest

		GPS waypoints
Start	Mabie Forest, off A710 Dumfries–New Abbey road	✎ NX 949 710
Distance	7¼ miles (11.6km)	Ⓐ NX 945 703
Height gain	1,295 feet (395m)	Ⓑ NX 935 699
Approximate time	4 hours	Ⓒ NX 931 707
Parking	Forestry Commission's Mabie Forest car park	Ⓓ NX 941 706
		Ⓔ NX 935 718
		Ⓕ NX 947 718
Ordnance Survey maps	Landranger 84 (Dumfries & Castle Douglas), Explorer 313 (Dumfries & Dalbeattie)	

If ever a forest contradicted the myth that woodland plantations are inevitably monotonous, it has to be Mabie Forest. This attractive and varied walk winds its way up and around wooded slopes above the River Nith. The woodland is mixed with plenty of broad-leaved trees, including 'Atlantic oakwood' where the characterful trees have convoluted branches covered in moss. At regular intervals superb views open up, sometimes across the Nith Estuary and Solway Firth, at other times looking inland towards Dumfries and the line of the Southern Uplands.

The route is waymarked, initially by brown-ringed posts then in the second half by yellow-ringed posts. The first part is mainly on surfaced paths, but the climb up Craigbill Hill is via a rocky and muddy path; the second part is largely on forest roads. You can cut the route in half (and do either the north or south part) by using paths through Dalshinnie Glen between the car park and Ⓓ. Many mountain bike routes criss-cross the woods, sometimes sharing forest roads with walkers. Take particular care where downhill trails cross your path, as riders may be travelling at speed.

✎ Start from the walks information board at the bottom of the car park on a path with multicoloured waymarker posts, soon turning left downhill. At

a signpost before the Mabie Burn footbridge turn left on an unmarked path (this is a shortcut). At a T-junction turn left following yellow, purple and brown markers uphill on a twisting path and at the next junction go right. Head uphill and cross a forest road.

When the path forks turn left and head uphill, now following only brown waymarkers. Cross a track and continue uphill. Keep ahead across another trail then walk more gently uphill with views over a field just outside the wood on the left. Level with the top of the field Ⓐ the path bends right and runs diagonally up through a more open area with naturally regenerating trees.

Turn right at a forest road then immediately left to continue uphill on the brown-waymarked path. Cross a downhill mountain bike trail and gradually weave uphill, entering characterful oak woodland, which is rich in primrose and other wildflowers in spring. The path now climbs over granite rock outcrops with muddy patches in between. At the top of a flight of steps with a handrail, a bench has superb views to the mouth of the Nith estuary. A good path now contours along Craigbill Hill to another bench looking towards the Solway Firth **B**.

The path gently loses height then zigzags down to a track running around the hillside. This glade catches the sun and is a prime spot for butterflies – all along are posts with photos of species you might see. There is a view left down to Lochaber Loch before you turn right at a T-junction along a forest road. At the crest fork left on another forest road. Follow it uphill for about 200m then look for a

path to the right **C**.

Follow the brown waymarkers and soon turn sharp right to head downhill below a felled area. Descend to a forest road and cross over then keep ahead to pass the left side of Dalshinnie Loch and a picnic table carved with dragonflies. The path soon bends left down to a path junction. Turn left and immediately come to another junction with a sign about Mabie Nature Reserve **D**.

Turn left, now following yellow-ringed posts. Within a few paces, the way divides in three. Take the middle path, which rises up to a forest road *(or to return to the car park turn right down Dalshinnie Glen)*. Turn right along the gradually ascending forest road through an area with open views. Crest the rise then turn right at a T-junction and gently descend to a minor crossroads of paths in a dip. Turn left downhill on a path under mature conifers.

At a major crossroads **E** meet a wide forest road and turn right along

Mabie View towards Kirkconnel Flow

```
0      200    400    600   800 METRES  1
                                         KILOMETRES
                                         MILES
0      200    400   600 YARDS    ½
```

it. Where the road bends right, fork left following yellow-marked posts along a boundary bank lined with massive beech trees. A covered bench on a knoll just off to the left has views to the north. Continue under the beeches until reaching a forest road then turn left along it. The road contours around Larch Hill, with more great views to the east from a bench at the top of Bauldie's Brae **F**.

Continue along the road, going around a long bend to the right with fields below. 'Mabie View', on the apex of the bend, looks over Kirconnell Flow. About 250 yds beyond the end of the fields, turn left down steps with a handrail. Cross a burn and bend left downstream. Just before the bottom, turn left at a yellow post and go down more steps and across a bridge. Follow the way downhill, ignoring paths to left and right, eventually bending right under giant redwoods to cross a stone bridge. Before a white house turn right up a tarmac drive, past the toilets and a picnic site, to cross the footbridge over Mabie Burn. Turn left then right back up to the car park. ●

Cairnsmore of Dee

		GPS waypoints
Start	Clatteringshaws Loch Wildlife Centre	🖉 NX 551 762
Distance	6 miles (9.7km)	Ⓐ NX 565 766
Height gain	1,705 feet (520m)	Ⓑ NX 566 759
Approximate time	4 hours	Ⓒ NX 583 757
Parking	Clatteringshaws Visitor Centre	Ⓓ NX 563 760
Ordnance Survey maps	Landranger 77 (Dalmellington & New Galloway), Explorer 319 (Galloway Forest Park South)	

Cairnsmore or Black Craig of Dee is the prominent hill seen to the south of the road between New Galloway and Clatteringshaws Loch. The first part of the walk from the shores of the loch to the summit of Benniguinea is an easy and gradual climb, mostly through forest, along wide, well-surfaced tracks. The second part from Benniguinea to the 1,616-ft (493m) summit of Cairnsmore of Dee crosses much rougher and more difficult terrain. There are splendid views throughout but this walk should not be undertaken in bad weather unless experienced in such conditions.

Clatteringshaws Visitor Centre (with **café**) is well worth a visit and, although not on our route, a path leads northwards from it to Bruce's Stone at Raploch Moss, commemorating a victory here by the Scottish king in 1307. Clatteringshaws Loch is a large reservoir created in 1931 as part of the Galloway hydro-electric scheme.

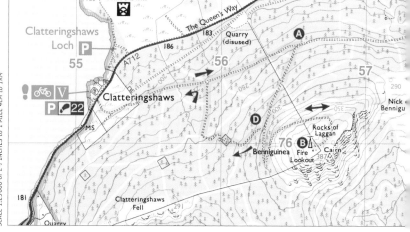

From the car park entrance cross the main road (A712) with good care and follow the forest road ahead. This surfaced track heads gently uphill across a field, curving to the left to meet a gate at the forest boundary. Go over a stile here and stay on the road passing below a wide swathe of clear-felled forest. Ignore the first turning on the right, at the far end of the cleared area, and then at the next junction turn sharp right **A** uphill. Ignore a path to the right **D** (the return route) and continue uphill. The track bends sharp left then curves around the north

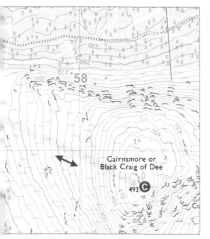

Clatteringshaws Loch

slopes of Benniguinea (1,269ft/387m) to the cairn and prominent mast on the summit **B**. The views, especially over Clatteringshaws Loch, are well worth the climb.

Retrace your steps for a few yards to the first bend and then head straight across towards Cairnsmore of Dee.

First descend into the col between the two peaks, by a young plantation on the left, and then head steeply up the ridge to the cairn and triangulation pillar on the summit **C**. The going is quite rough underfoot – no visible path, coarse and tussocky grass, rocky, heathery, and with soft ground and mud in places. However, the extensive panoramic views more than compensate for the effort.

On the return journey, after the sharp right bend below Benniguinea, turn left **D** to head downhill on a rough but well-surfaced footpath. Follow this through the remains of a stone enclosure to reach a forest road. Turn right along this road and at the next junction turn left to follow the road back to the car park.

Sweetheart Abbey and Criffel

Start	New Abbey
Distance	6½ miles (10.6km)
Height gain	2,015 feet (615m)
Approximate time	4½ hours
Parking	New Abbey
Ordnance Survey maps	Landranger 84 (Dumfries & Castle Douglas), Explorer 313 (Dumfries & Dalbeattie)

GPS waypoints

- 🖉 NX 964 663
- **A** NX 961 660
- **B** NX 957 654
- **C** NX 955 648
- **D** NX 955 631
- **E** NX 957 618
- **F** NX 961 651

Rising abruptly above the western side of the Nith Estuary, the conical shaped, isolated hill of Criffel is one of the most distinctive and easily recognisable landmarks on the Solway coast. Although of relatively modest height, (1,868ft/569m), the ascent from New Abbey, which starts virtually from sea level, is both lengthy and continuous and certainly gives the impression that you have climbed much higher. Not surprisingly, the views from the summit are superb, extending to the Isle of Man on clear days. Muddy conditions can be expected in places and this walk is not recommended in bad weather unless you are experienced and equipped for such conditions.

Dominating the very attractive village of New Abbey are the imposing, red sandstone ruins of Sweetheart Abbey. This 'new abbey' was founded in 1273 and gets its name because its foundress, Devorgilla, was so fond of her husband, John Balliol, that she kept his embalmed heart after his death and had it buried with her in the abbey after she died in 1290.

Although few of the domestic buildings survive, the church, which dates from the 13th and 14th centuries, is almost complete apart from the roof and windows. Particularly impressive is the west front, nave and central tower.

🖉 Start in the Square and, facing the **Abbey Arms**, take the road to the right. At a sign 'Pedestrian Way to Waterloo Monument' turn left along a tarmac drive, by the pond of an 18th-century corn mill on the right, and follow it around a right bend. Look out for some steps on the left, climb them and walk along a narrow path.

Go through a kissing-gate, keep ahead by the left edge of a field to go through another gate and climb a stile to rejoin the tarmac drive **A**. Continue along the drive for about ½ mile (800m). The Waterloo Monument, begun in 1815, the year of the battle, can be seen to the right. Where the drive ends there is a fork ahead. Turn

Sweetheart Abbey

left **B** and cross a bridge over the Glen Burn indicated by a signpost to Criffel 2½ miles. Keep ahead and pass a cottage. At a second cottage the path passes on its right. In summer this can be fairly overgrown with bracken and you will have to push through. Keep on this path until it reaches a forest road **C** then turn right.

Follow the track around a left bend but at a right bend turn left onto a narrow footpath through the trees. Keep to it as it curves to the right then follows a firebreak on the long and steady climb uphill with a wall on the left. Cross, first of all, a wall and then a stile over a wire fence.

At the right bend turn left onto a narrow footpath through the trees and keep on it as it curves to the right and follows a firebreak uphill with a wall on the left-hand side. Keep following it upside crossing a wall then a wire fence to keep ahead on the indistinct but visible path that bisects the wall and fence, heading steeply uphill to the cairn on the 1,476-ft (450m) summit of Knockendoch **D**. The superb all-round views are simply a taste of what is to come.

Criffel is straight ahead. The path bears right and you follow it along a ridge, curving gradually left in an arc, to the triangulation pillar on the summit **E**. The views are tremendous and include the Solway coast, Cumbrian mountains, Nith Estuary, Sweetheart Abbey, Loch Kindar and the line of the Southern Uplands. In very clear conditions the Isle of Arran and Isle of Man can be seen.

Retrace your steps back over Knockendoch and down to the forest track. On the descent there are more enjoyable views of Loch Kindar, Sweetheart Abbey and the Solway. Turn right along the track but instead of shortly turning left to continue on the outward route **C**, stay on it and head gently downhill to a metal gate. Go through the gate, walk through a plantation and go through a metal gate at the far end. Continue across a field, go through a metal gate and cross a footbridge over a burn **F**. The track swings right, passes through another metal gate and continues along the left inside edge of woodland.

Go through a metal gate, walk along an enclosed track, go through another gate and continue by a wall on the left, soon bending left to go through yet another metal gate. Continue along a track and bear right through green gates to reach the edge of a new housing estate.

Just before reaching a road, turn left along a track and where it bends left, turn right over a stone stile. Continue along a footpath through trees and by garden fences on the right. Turn right at a public footpath fingerpost, go down some steps then keep left to go through a gap in the wall, down some more steps and continue along the path. At a T-junction with a lane head diagonally right across it to continue along a concrete path between a wall on the left and a wire fence on the right. When you reach the main road cross it then turn left, passing the **Abbey Cottage Tearoom** on the way back to the car park.

Cairnsmore of Fleet

Start	Cairnsmore Estate car park. From the A75 take the unsigned road south-east of Palnure (just south of the bridge over Palnure Burn) and keep left at the entrance to Cairnsmore. The next turn, a sharp right, leads to the car parking bays
Distance	7½ miles (12.2km)
Height gain	2,295 feet (700m)
Approximate time	4½ hours
Parking	Cairnsmore Estate car park
Ordnance Survey maps	Landranger 83 (Newton Stewart & Kirkcudbright), Explorer 319 (Galloway Forest Park South)

GPS waypoints

- ✎ NX 463 632
- Ⓐ NX 473 642
- Ⓑ NX 492 654
- Ⓒ NX 501 670

Although Cairnsmore of Fleet is among the higher Galloway hills (2,331ft/711m), the ascent of it could hardly be easier or more straightforward and on a fine day it would be an ideal introduction for anyone who has not scaled such heights before. The climb is steady, with no difficult or strenuous stretches, the path is clear throughout and the views over the Galloway hills, Cree Estuary and Solway coast are magnificent.

✎ Go through a gate at the far end of the car park, turn left onto a driveway and continue uphill, crossing a bridge over Cairnsmore Burn. Turn right onto a footpath marked by a yellow waymarker and 'Hill Walk' sign. When the path reaches a track turn left beside another yellow waymarker. Keep straight ahead to the track end then go through a metal gate into a field. Walk diagonally uphill across it to a similar gate in the top left corner Ⓐ. Just beyond go through a wooden gate into the conifer forest. Keep on a

Cairnsmore of Fleet

Memorial on summit of Cairnsmore of Fleet

Retrace your steps downhill to the start, enjoying more splendid views across the Cree Estuary below.

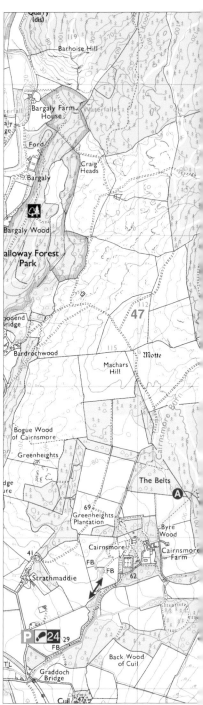

well trodden footpath heading uphill. Go through a gap in a stone wall and continue following the path, with views over a clear-felled area on the left to the Galloway Hills. Cross a forest road by a memorial seat to Rosemary Pilkington and keep on uphill, eventually emerging from the trees onto open hillside. Ahead the path can be clearly seen, ascending the grassy and heathery slopes of Cairnsmore of Fleet. Crossing the path a short distance ahead is a fence and a gate **B**. Cross this by a ladder-stile to the right. The path now winds uphill more steeply. Near the top it flattens out and follows a line of cairns to the memorial stone, erected to the memory of all airmen killed in aircraft crashes on the mountain in the Second World War.

Just beyond is the summit cairn and triangulation pillar **C** from where there are magnificent views over the Galloway hills (including Merrick), Cree Estuary, Wigtown and Luce Bays, the Machars, Mull of Galloway and, in clear conditions, the Isle of Man, Cumbrian fells and Northern Ireland.

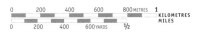

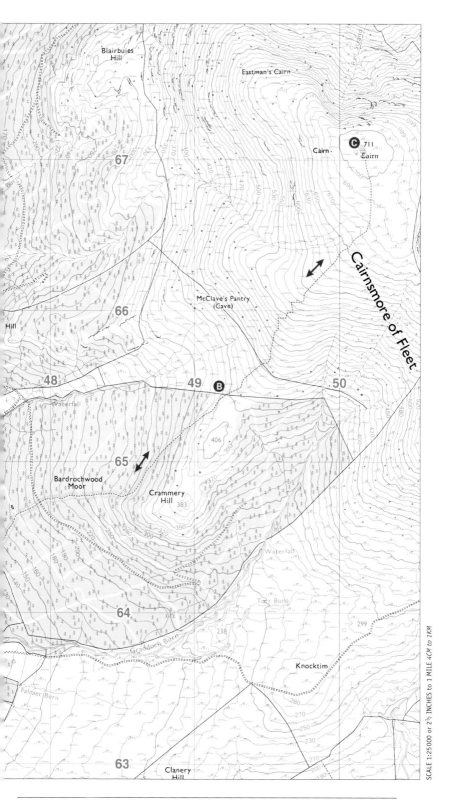

Blairbuies
Hill

Eastman's Cairn

Cairn

C 711
Cairn

67

Cairnsmore of Fleet

McClave's Pantry
(Cave)

66

Hill

48

49

B

50

Waterfall

406

65

Bardrochwood
Moor

Crammery
Hill 383

470

350

320

300

280

Waterfall

Tonr Burn

64

238

299

Craddoch Burn

Knocktim

Falmaer Burn

280

270

250

230

210

200

190

63

Clanery
Hill

SCALE 1:25000 or 2½ INCHES to 1 MILE 4CM to 1KM

Black Hill and Well Hill

Start	Durisdeer
Distance	5½ miles (8.9km)
Height gain	1,855ft (565m)
Approximate time	4 hours
Parking	By the church and war memorial at Durisdeer
Ordnance Survey maps	Landranger 78 (Nithsdale & Annandale), Explorer 329 (Lowther Hills, Sanquhar & Leadhills)

GPS waypoints

- ⬗ NS 893 037
- Ⓐ NS 895 038
- Ⓑ NS 894 058
- Ⓒ NS 913 064
- Ⓓ NS 915 059

Despite a relatively modest height of 1,744ft (531m), the initial climb to the summit of Black Hill is hard work: steep, long – 1¼ miles (2km) – pathless and over rough terrain. Once the triangulation pillar is reached, the going becomes easier as you descend into a col and then steadily climb again to the higher summit of Well Hill (1,987ft/606m). Then comes a very steep descent to a track, followed by a relaxing finale as you gently descend along this track, the Well Path, an ancient routeway that dates back to Roman times. The views over Nithsdale and the Lowther Hills from the higher points are magnificent. As you are dependent on certain landmarks, this walk should on no account be attempted in bad weather, especially misty conditions.

It is surprising to find such a large and elegant church in a village as small as Durisdeer. The reason is that it was built by the first Duke of Queensberry of nearby Drumlanrig Castle and the north wing was the Queensberry mausoleum. The church dates from 1699 and retains the old box pews.

⬗ Begin by taking the lane to the right of Durisdeer church after passing between cottages and going through a metal gate, by a signpost 'Wald Path to Traloss' and onto a rough track. This is the Well Path, an ancient route through the hills. Of Roman origin, it was later used by medieval pilgrims, including several Scottish kings, on their way to

the shrine of St Ninian at Whithorn.

You soon leave the Well Path by turning left through the first metal gate Ⓐ. and descending steeply to cross a small bridge over Kirk Burn. This might be difficult after wet weather. Head up the other side, pass through a wall gap and climb steeply over the hill ahead. To the right are fine views up the valley of Kirk Burn and behind, Durisdeer church can be seen half hidden by a circle of trees, with Nithsdale in the distance. At the top descend into a col to reach a gate in a wire fence just to the left of a circular enclosure. Go through and now climb more steeply across rough grass and

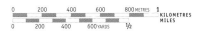

heather up the flanks of Black Hill.
After the final steep pull up to the
summit plateau, head across to the
triangulation pillar **B**. The magnificent
panoramic views include Criffel on the
Solway coast, the main Galloway range,
the Lowther Hills and the Border hills.

At the triangulation pillar turn right
and descend across rough grass, later
making for and keeping by a wire fence
on the left. In the col between Black
Hill and Well Hill turn left through a
gate and turn right to continue uphill
again, now with a wire fence on the
right. Keep by this fence – there is
later a parallel wall as well – around
right and left bends, climbing to the
summit of Well Hill **C**, another superb
viewpoint.

At the summit turn right through
a gate and descend steeply, keeping
beside a wire fence and wall on the
right, to a track. Turn right **D**, go

through a gate and follow this track gently downhill through a pass in the hills to return to the start. The actual Well Path runs parallel just below in the valley on the right and as you descend, the outline of a Roman fort can be seen beside it. A little farther on the Well Path joins the track and you keep along it for the last ½ mile (800m) into Durisdeer.

Durisdeer church

Caldons Burn and Lamachan Hill

		GPS waypoints
Start	Bridge over the River Trool 1½ miles (2.4km) east of Glen Trool Visitor Centre at Stroan Bridge	🖉 NX 397 791
		Ⓐ NX 415 775
Distance	8½ miles (13.7km)	Ⓑ NX 435 770
		Ⓒ NX 429 762
Height gain	2,380 feet (725m)	Ⓓ NX 403 767
Approximate time	5½ hours	Ⓔ NX 413 777
Parking	There is space for several cars on a hard standing area beside the bridge	
Ordnance Survey maps	Landranger 77 (Dalmellington & New Galloway), Explorer 319 (Galloway Forest Park South)	

Lamachan Hill is the highest peak in the Minnigaff range that lies to the south of Loch Trool and is flanked by Larg Hill to the west and Bennanbrack to the east. A delightful, though rocky and sometimes muddy walk beside Caldons Burn through the forest leads on to the open hillside for a steady climb to the 2,350-ft (717m) summit. From here there are stunning views. The return descends to the col between Lamachan Hill and Larg Hill, and continues over the top of Craignaw to re-enter the forest and rejoin Caldons Burn. This walk should not be attempted in bad, especially misty, weather, unless experienced in such conditions and able to navigate by using a compass.

🖉 From the car park cross the bridge into the former Caldons Campsite and follow the drive to a bridge. Turn right before the bridge and follow a faint track along the river bank.

Continue along the winding path through the trees. Since the closure of Caldons Campsite the path has become a bit overgrown with bracken and occasionally briar. A stout stick or a walking pole comes in useful on this section for clearing a way through.

In addition the going can be difficult with wet, muddy and rocky sections not to mention overhanging branches. The path is also very faint in parts but that's not such a problem as you just need to follow the course of the burn and keep taking the line of least resistance. The occasional stretch of duckboarding will help keep you on line.

After ½ mile (800m) cross a stile. It's a bit less overgrown from here but still has lots of boggy sections to negotiate.

In a farther ¼ mile (400m) cross a ruined dyke and continue uphill along the edge of an interesting little gorge. The path crosses a forest road and the going gets a bit easier from then. Head inland a bit from the burn to follow the line of a wall. Cross the wall then head steeply up hill to emerge in a clearing

with a grand view of a waterfall before you. This can be rather spectacular after heavy rainfall.

Continue along the edge of the burn to meet and ford the Mulmein Burn, a tributary of Caldons Ⓐ.

Now cross a wall on the left and continue by the wall on the right. Cross a wire fence, turn left to ford Caldons Burn, cross another wall and turn right to continue uphill, by a wall on the

On the summit of Craignaw

right. Soon you emerge from the forest and head more steeply uphill, between Cambrick Hill to the left and Craignaw to the right. Ford a burn and continue climbing, keeping by the wall on the right all the while, to the summit cairn on Lamachan Hill **B**. From here there are splendid all-round views over the Galloway hills.

At the cairn turn right and follow a line of iron fence posts gently down-

hill into the col between Lamachan Hill and Larg Hill which lies ahead **C**. Turn right and continue downhill, initially by a wall on the left but later bearing away from the wall in the direction of the prominent bulk of Craignaw, seen on the ascent. Descend into a dip and then climb quite steeply to the summit cairn (1,772ft/540m). Behind is a striking view of the Larg Hill-Lamachan Hill-Bennanbrack ridge.

Continue along the ridge – there are a number of 'ups and downs' – over rough, tussocky grass and bear left towards the edge of the conifers below. On this part of the walk you may be lucky enough to see some wild goats. Turn left at the corner of the forest and follow a grassy ride steeply downhill to a track **D**. Turn right along it, passing a disused quarry, and the track bears right. Then keep ahead along the right-hand edge of a clear-felled area, to emerge on to the path above Caldons Burn **E**.

Turn left and retrace your steps downhill beside the burn to the starting point.

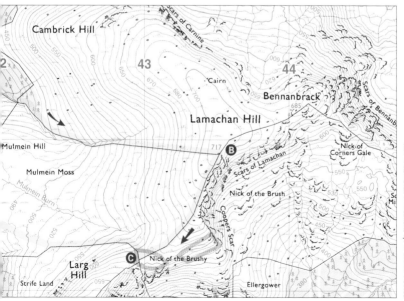

SCALE 1:25 000 or 2½ INCHES to 1 MILE 4CM to 1KM

Colvend Coast

		GPS waypoints
Start	Kippford	✐ NX 836 553
Distance	10 miles (16.1km)	Ⓐ NX 837 549
Height gain	835ft (255m)	Ⓑ NX 847 537
Approximate time	5 hours	Ⓒ NX 849 536
Parking	Kippford	Ⓓ NX 854 524
		Ⓔ NX 880 536
Ordnance Survey maps	Landranger 84	Ⓕ NX 880 546
	(Dumfries & Castle Douglas),	Ⓖ NX 868 545
	Explorer 313	Ⓗ NX 857 563
	(Dumfries & Dalbeattie)	Ⓙ NX 851 554

Colvend refers to the stretch of the Solway coast between Rough Firth and Sandyhills Bay. It is an outstandingly attractive and spectacular coastline but the inland part of the walk, mainly through forest, is scarcely any less enjoyable and there is a succession of splendid views throughout. This is a lengthy and quite energetic walk, particularly the section along the coast path, but a highly memorable one, especially on a fine and clear day, and well worth taking plenty of time over.

In the 19th century, Kippford had a busy ship repair and building yard but the River Urr silted up and now it has become a popular boating centre and small resort.

✐ Turn left out of the car park and walk down the road alongside the Urr Estuary. At the building with a post box turn left (No Through Road sign) up a narrow lane Ⓐ, signposted Jubilee Path, which bends to the right and then heads uphill.

After passing the last of the houses, continue along a rocky path – there is a National Trust for Scotland sign 'Jubilee Path to Rockcliffe' – between gorse and trees. At a meeting of paths and tracks, keep ahead along a straight, wooded, enclosed track which later becomes a tarmac track. Follow the track around a sharp right bend

down into the quiet coastal village of Rockcliffe and turn left alongside the beach Ⓑ.

At a footpath sign 'To Castle Point' turn right Ⓒ along a tarmac drive. To the right are attractive views of Rockcliffe, Rough Firth and the River Urr, with hills framing the background. At a National Trust for Scotland sign 'Footpath to Castle Point and Sandyhills', turn right on to a path that winds alternately between bushes and along the rocky shore to reach Nelson's Grave. This is nothing to do with Admiral Lord Nelson but the grave of Joseph Nelson of Whitehaven who was drowned at sea in 1791. Just after passing the grave climb a stone stile, continue along the path following the edge of a field and at the end of it keep straight ahead to climb to the magnificent viewpoint of Castlehill , site of an ancient fort dating from around 400BC. A toposcope enables you to identify the range of places that can be seen from here on a clear day. Follow the other path back downhill then turn right and walk round the edge of the field before turning right to cross a stone stile by a fingerpost then continue along the coastal path.

Now follows a superb stretch of coastal walking; the path hugs the coast and keeps along the cliffs all the way, there are regular 'Coastal Path' signs and a number of stiles. This is quite an energetic part of the walk with several steep climbs and descents but the scenery is outstanding. Keep a look out for a memorial just off the path to the captain of the Schooner Elbe who landed his crew here before sinking. Eventually, the path drops down to the handful of charming cottages at Port O'Warren Bay, descending a flight of steps to a stone stile.

Climb the stile and turn left uphill , in the Portling, Douglas Hall and Sandyhills direction. Later, the track becomes a lane which descends to the whitewashed hamlet of Portling. Ignore a footpath sign to the right and keep ahead along the lane to a road . Turn left – take care as this road can be busy – for ¾ mile (1.2km) into Colvend.

Take the path on the right to Barcloy Hill and Long Distance Path to Dalbeattie  along a track that passes to the right of the village hall. The track passes houses and heads gently uphill to enter woodland. Continue through the trees to pass by Barean Loch and keep ahead, keeping left where the path is joined by another near two waymarkers. At the next

Looking back along the Solway coast at Barcloy Hill

junction by another two waymarks keep left again then keep a look out for another waymarker just before a junction. On the far side of this waymarker is an arrow pointing to the A710. Turn left into a footpath here

H. Go through a gate and walk along the left edge of rough pasture with a wire fence and later a wall on the left. When you reach the end of the field by a cottage turn right along the wall to find a gate leading to a footpath which

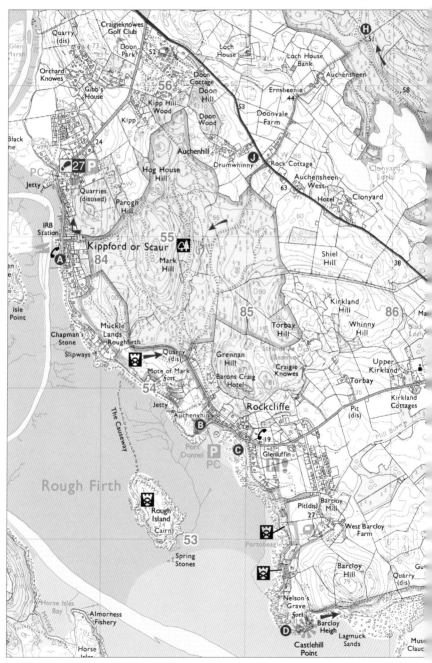

will take you round the cottage and through another gate onto a tarmac lane. Turn right onto this and follow it to the A710.

Turn left and then immediately right  on to a track and pass beside a gate. Continue along this very pleasant track, through woodland.

At the first junction go right, continue uphill to a T-junction and turn right again. At the next junction turn left and continue uphill following the blue waymarker poles. When the path heads downhill to a crossroads keep straight ahead then keep your eyes peeled for a faint path branching off to the right at a blue waymarker. Turn right and head downhill through the woods on a narrow path. The path winds downhill through trees and around several sharp bends to emerge on to a track. Continue down into Kippford and at the bottom turn right along the road to return to the car park.

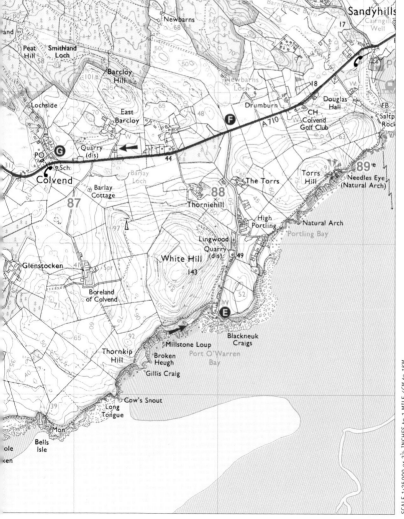

SCALE 1:25000 or 2½ INCHES to 1 MILE 4CM to 1KM

Merrick

		GPS waypoints	
Start	Bruce's Stone, at the end of minor road on north side of Loch Trool	🖋 NX 415 804	
		Ⓐ NX 420 804	
Distance	9½ miles (15.3km)	Ⓑ NX 442 846	
Height gain	2,575 feet (785m)	Ⓒ NX 427 855	
Approximate time	6½ hours	Ⓓ NX 414 838	
Parking	Bruce's Stone	Ⓔ NX 414 823	
Ordnance Survey maps	Landranger 77 (Dalmellington & New Galloway), Explorer 318 (Galloway Forest Park North)		

At 2,766ft (843m), the summit of Merrick is the highest point in southern Scotland. The ascent is a strenuous and challenging one and its difficulties should not be under-estimated. Allow plenty of time for the walk and it should only be attempted by reasonably fit and experienced walkers. *The path by Gairland Burn – rocky and difficult in places and often muddy and waterlogged – leads past a succession of lochs to reach the shores of Loch Enoch. From here comes a very steep climb of almost one mile (1.6km) to the summit, from where you enjoy the most magnificent views. The descent is much easier along a well-marked path all the way. A possible alternative for less experienced walkers is to do a 'there and back' walk using the clear and well-used return route in reverse to reach the summit.* It must be emphasised that this walk up Merrick should definitely not be embarked upon in poor weather conditions, especially during the winter months.

Bruce's Stone, a magnificent viewpoint overlooking Loch Trool, was erected to commemorate a victory by Robert the Bruce over the English in 1307.

🖋 From the parking bay, take the path for Bruce's Stone. Facing the stone and loch, turn left along a track, ignoring the footpath sign to Merrick unless doing the 'there and back' alternative route. The track bends right, heads downhill and bends left to cross a bridge over Buchan Burn.

Keep ahead on the road, go through a kissing-gate then when the road bends to the right beside a gate go over a stile Ⓐ, signposted to Gairland Burn and Loch Valley. Head uphill, go through a gate, continue initially by a wall on the left and go through another gate. Now keep by the wall on the right and the path soon bears left across the bouldery slopes of Buchan Hill above Gairland Burn. Later, it descends to keep beside the burn – a lovely stretch of the walk

– to reach Loch Valley. Walk along the left shore of the loch and continue beside the burn again to the beautiful, rugged and lonely shores of Loch Neldricken.

Keep along the left bank – the path becomes indistinct here – passing the infamous 'Murder Hole', a small bay at the far western corner featured in S.R. Crockett's novel *The Raiders*. Apparently, the water never freezes over here.

Bear right at the corner of the loch and head up to pass through a wall gap. Continue uphill, by a burn on the right, passing to the left of the crags of Ewe Rig. Over to the right the small Loch Arron is seen and the route continues through a pass at Craig Neldricken to descend to the shores of the wild, beautiful and island-studded Loch Enoch **B**. Merrick rears up to the left, a daunting sight.

Turn left beside the loch, pass over a low wall and wire fence in the south

Loch Neldricken

west corner and now head up the grassy slopes to the summit of Merrick. The ascent is steep and tiring but the terrain is not difficult. After the final steep pull up to the plateau, it is with relief and a great feeling of satisfaction that you head across to the summit cairn and triangulation pillar **C**. The outstanding panoramic views across mountains and lochs and over to Ailsa Craig on the Ayrshire coast extend, in clear weather, to the Isle of Man, Lakeland fells and the Antrim coast of Northern Ireland.

At the summit turn left and head steadily downhill, in a south-westerly direction, across the smooth, grassy plateau, following a series of cairns, towards the clear ridge ahead, called the Neive of the Spit. Later, you join and keep by a wall on the right to head gently uphill along the ridge over the summit of Benyellary (2,362ft/720m) **D**.

Continue past the summit cairn, descending more steeply and still with the wall on the right. In front, the views looking towards Glen Trool are superb.

The path later veers left away from the wall down to a kissing-gate. Go through, head down to the edge of the forest and continue quite steeply downhill between conifers to a track. Turn right, cross a bridge over Whiteland Burn and immediately turn left **E**, to continue downhill. The path bears right and winds through the trees, emerging from the forest at a kissing-gate.

Go through the gate and keep ahead above Buchan Burn for a most attractive finale with grand views ahead over Loch Trool to the forested slopes beyond. Go through another kissing-gate and the path leads down to the start. ●

SCALE 1:25000 or 2½ INCHES to 1 MILE 4CM to 1KM

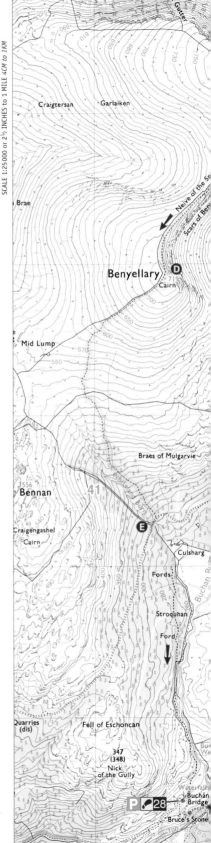

Further Information

 ## Walkers and the Law

Walkers in Scotland have long enjoyed a moral and de facto right of access. Nothing much has changed except that this is now enshrined in *The Land Reform (Scotland) Act 2003*. The Act tells you where you have right of access and *The Scottish Outdoor Access Code* sets out your responsibilities when exercising your rights. These rights came into effect on 9 February 2005.

Walkers following the routes in this book should not have any problems but it is as well to know something about the law as it affects access, particularly as the legislation in Scotland is significantly different from elsewhere in Britain. Mostly, though, it's just common sense. Be considerate to other land users, look after the places you visit and take responsibility for your own safety.

The Scottish Outdoor Access Code

1. Take responsibility for your own actions.
2. Respect people's privacy and peace of mind. When close to a house or garden, keep a sensible distance from the house, use a path or track if there is one, and take extra care at night.
3. Help land managers and others to work safely and effectively. Do not hinder land management operations and follow advice from land managers. Respect requests for reasonable limitations on when and where you can go.
4. Care for your environment. Do not disturb wildlife, leave the environment as you find it and follow a path or track if there is one.
5. Keep your dog under proper control. Do not take it through fields of calves and lambs, and dispose of dog dirt.
6. Take extra care if you are organising an event or running a business and ask the landowner's advice.
Some fairly comprehensive guidance is available at:
www.outdooraccess-scotland.com

The following covers some of the most common situations affecting walkers.

Car Parking
Motorised vehicles are not included in the access rights, but most people will use a vehicle to reach the start of a walk. It's important to park sensibly and avoid causing an obstruction. Use a car park if one is nearby. If not, make sure you do not block the entrance to a field or building, make it difficult for other road users or damage the verge.

Dogs
Dog walkers are covered by the legislation provided they keep their dogs under control at all times. Avoid fields with sheep during the lambing season (spring). During the bird-breeding season (April – July) keep your dog on a lead while near breeding habitats. Where crossing fields containing animals keep your dog on a short lead.

Farm Steadings
There is no legal right of access to farm steadings. In practice though many tracks and paths do go through farm steadings and you should consider the following advice:
If a right of way or core path goes through the steading then you can follow that.
If an alternative route has been signposted round the steading then it should be used. If the route through the steading has been taken on a customary basis you may be able to continue to do so.
You may go through the steading if the farmer gives you permission. Otherwise you will have to exercise your legal right to go around the farm steading and buildings.
Whatever route you use through, or round, a farm steading exercise care, avoid machinery and livestock and respect the privacy of people living on the farm.

Fields
Keep to paths where possible or walk

Glossary of Gaelic Names

Many of the place names in Scotland are Gaelic in origin, and this list gives some of the more common elements, which will allow readers to understand otherwise meaningless words and appreciate the relationship between place names and landscape features. Place names often have variant spellings, and the more common of these are given here.

aber	mouth of loch, river	eilidh	hind
abhainn	river	eòin, eun	bird
allt	stream	fionn	white
auch, ach	field	fraoch	heather
bal, bail, baile	town, homestead	gabhar, ghabhar,	
bàn	white, fair, pale	gobhar	goat
bealach	hill pass	garbh	rough
beg, beag	small	geal	white
ben, beinn	hill	ghlas, glas	grey
bhuidhe	yellow	gleann, glen	narrow, valley
blar	plain	gorm	blue, green
brae, braigh	upper slope, steepening	inbhir, inver	confluence
		inch, inis, innis	island, meadow by river
breac	speckled		
cairn	pile of stones, often marking a summit	lag, laggan	hollow
		làrach	old site
cam	crooked	làirig	pass
càrn	cairn, cairn-shaped hill	leac	slab
		liath	grey
caol, kyle	strait	loch	lake
ceann, ken, kin	head	lochan	small loch
cil, kil	church, cell	màm	pass, rise
clach	stone	maol	bald-shaped top
clachan	small village	monadh	upland, moor
cnoc	hill, knoll, knock	mór, mor(e)	big
coille, killie	wood	odhar, odhair	dun-coloured
corrie, coire, choire	mountain hollow	rhu, rubha	point
		ruadh	red, brown
craig, creag	cliff, crag	sgòr, sgòrr, sgùrr	pointed
crannog, crannag	man-made island	sron	nose
dàl, dail	field, flat	stob	pointed
damh	stag	strath	valley (broader than glen)
dearg	red		
druim, drum	long ridge	tarsuinn	traverse, across
dubh, dhu	black, dark	tom	hillock (rounded)
dùn	hill fort	tòrr	hillock (more rugged)
eas	waterfall	tulloch, tulach	knoll
eilean	island	uisge	water, river

around the margins of a field under crops. Bear in mind that grass is also grown as a crop. Where fields have been sprayed there are occasions when the landowner has a responsibility to keep people out for health and safety reasons for anything from a few hours to three or four days. Obey any signs or advice from the landowner and work out an alternative route, perhaps through an adjacent field.

Golf Courses

You have a right of access to cross golf courses, but must avoid damage to the playing surface and never step onto the greens. Cross as quickly as possible but consider the rights of the players at the same time. Wait for players to play their shot before crossing the fairway; if you're close to someone about to play, stop and stand still. Keep to any paths that exist and keep dogs on a short lead.

Deer Stalking

During the hunting season walkers should check to ensure that the walks they are planning avoid deer stalking operations.

Culling is an essential part of the management of a sustainable deer population and to avoid overgrazing and damage to fragile habitats.

The red stag stalking season is from 1 July to 20 October, hinds are culled from 21 October to 15 February. September and October tend to be the busiest months. The roe buck stalking season is from 1 April to 20 October, with June to August seeing the peak of activity. The doe-stalking season is from 21 October to 31 March.

During the busy periods of the season stalking can take place six days of the week but never on a Sunday.

The easiest way to find out if the walk you are planning is affected is to refer to the Hillphones website www.snh.org.uk/hillphones. Here you can find a map of the phones and the relevant numbers. Calls are charged at normal rates and you will hear a recorded message that is changed each morning.

Grouse Shooting

The season runs from 12 August to 10 December. During this period please follow any advice regarding alternative routes on grouse moors to minimise disturbance to the shoot. Avoid crossing land where a shoot is in progress until it is absolutely safe to do so.

 Safety on the Hills

The hills, mountains and moorlands of Britain, though of modest height compared with those in many other countries, need to be treated with respect. Friendly and inviting in good weather, they can quickly be transformed into wet, misty, windswept and potentially dangerous areas of wilderness in bad weather. Even on an outwardly fine and settled summer day, conditions can rapidly deteriorate at high altitudes and, in winter, even more so.

Therefore it is advisable to always take both warm and waterproof clothing, sufficient nourishing food, a hot drink, first-aid kit, torch and whistle. Wear suitable footwear, such as strong walking boots or shoes that give a good grip over rocky terrain and on slippery slopes. Try to obtain a local weather forecast and bear it in mind before you start. Do not be afraid to abandon your proposed route and return to your starting point in the event of a sudden and unexpected deterioration in the weather. Do not go alone and allow enough time to finish the walk well before nightfall.

Most of the walks described in this book do not venture into remote wilderness areas and will be safe to do, given due care and respect, at any time of year in all but the most unreasonable weather. Indeed, a crisp, fine winter day often provides perfect walking conditions, with firm ground underfoot and a clarity that is not possible to achieve in the other seasons of the year. A few walks, however, are suitable only for reasonably fit and experienced hill walkers able to use a compass and should definitely not be tackled by anyone else during the winter months or in bad weather, especially high winds and mist. These are indicated in the general description that precedes each of the walks.

 Useful Organisations

Association for the Protection of Rural Scotland
Dolphin House, 4 Hunter Square, Edinburgh, EH1 1QW
Tel. 0131 225 7012
www.aprs.scot

Dumfries and Galloway Council
Council Offices, English Street,
Dumfries DG1 2DD
Tel. 0303 333 3000
www.dumgal.gov.uk

Forestry Commission Scotland
Silvan House, 231 Corstorphine Road,
Edinburgh EH12 7AT
Tel. 0300 067 6156
www.scotland.forestry.gov.uk

Historic Environment Scotland
Longmore House, Salisbury Place,
Edinburgh EH9 1SH
Tel. 0131 668 8600
www.historicenvironment.scot

Long Distance Walkers' Association
www.ldwa.org.uk

National Trust for Scotland
Hermiston Quay, 5 Cultins Road,
Edinburgh, EH11 4DF
Tel. 0131 458 0200
www.nts.org.uk

Ordnance Survey
Tel. 03456 05 05 05
www.ordnancesurvey.co.uk

Ramblers Scotland
Caledonia House, 1 Redheughs
Rigg, South Gyle, Edinburgh, EH12 9DQ
Tel. 0131 472 7006
www.ramblers.org.uk/scotland

Scottish Natural Heritage
Great Glen House, Leachkin Road,
Inverness IV3 8NW
Tel. 01463 725000
www.snh.scot

Scottish Rights of Way & Access Society
24 Annandale Street, Edinburgh EH7 4AN
Tel. 0131 558 1222
www.scotways.com

Scottish Land and Estates
Stuart House, Eskmills Business Park
Musselburgh EH21 7PB
Tel. 0131 653 5400
www.scottishlandandestates.co.uk

Scottish Wildlife Trust
Harbourside House, 110 Commercial Street,

Edinburgh, EH6 6NF
Tel. 0131 312 7765
www.scottishwildlifetrust.org.uk

Scottish Youth Hostels Assocation
7 Glebe Crescent, Stirling
FK8 2JA
Tel. 01786 891400
www.syha.org.uk

Visit Scotland Dumfries and Galloway
www.visitscotland.com

Local tourist information offices
Dumfries: 01387 253862
Gretna Green: 01461 335208
Kirkcudbright: 01557 330494
Stranraer: 01776 702595

 Ordnance Survey maps of Dumfries and Galloway

Dumfries and Galloway is covered by
Ordnance Survey 1:50 000 (11/4 inches to 1
mile or 2cm to 1km) scale Landranger map
sheets 71, 76, 77, 78, 79, 82, 83, 84 and 85.
These all-purpose maps are packed with
information to help you explore the area.
Viewpoints, picnic sites, places of interest
and caravan and camping sites are shown,
as well as public rights of way information
such as footpaths and bridleways.

To examine the Dumfries and Galloway
area in more detail, Ordnance Survey
Explorer maps at 1:25 000 scale (2½ inches
to 1 mile or 4cm to 1km) are ideal:

309 Stranraer & The Rhins
310 Glenluce & Kirkcowan
311 Wigtown, Whithorn & The Machars
312 Kirkcudbright & Castle Douglas
313 Dumfries & Dalbeattie
318 Galloway Forest Park North
319 Galloway Forest Park South
320 Castle Douglas, Loch Ken & New Galloway
321 Nithsdale & Dumfries
322 Annandale
323 Eskdale & Castle O'er Forest
328 Sanquhar & New Cumnock
329 Lowther Hills, Sanquhar & Leadhills
330 Moffat & St Mary's Loch

Further Information

Ordnance Survey

 Pathfinder® Guides | **Britain's best-loved walking guides**

Scotland
Pathfinder Walks
3 ISLE OF SKYE
4 CAIRNGORMS
7 FORT WILLIAM & GLEN COE
19 DUMFRIES & GALLOWAY
23 LOCH LOMOND, THE TROSSACHS, & STIRLING
27 PERTHSHIRE, ANGUS & FIFE
30 LOCH NESS & INVERNESS
31 OBAN, MULL & KINTYRE
46 ABERDEEN & ROYAL DEESIDE
47 EDINBURGH, PENTLANDS & LOTHIANS

North of England
Pathfinder Walks
15 YORKSHIRE DALES
22 MORE LAKE DISTRICT
28 NORTH YORK MOORS
35 NORTHUMBERLAND & the SCOTTISH BORDERS
39 DURHAM, NORTH PENNINES & TYNE AND WEAR
42 CHESHIRE
49 VALE OF YORK & YORKSHIRE WOLDS
53 LANCASHIRE
60 LAKE DISTRICT
63 PEAK DISTRICT
64 SOUTH PENNINES
71 THE HIGH FELLS OF LAKELAND
73 MORE PEAK DISTRICT

Short Walks
1 YORKSHIRE DALES
2 PEAK DISTRICT
3 LAKE DISTRICT
13 NORTH YORK MOORS
20 CHESHIRE & THE GRITSTONE EDGE

Wales
Pathfinder Walks
10 SNOWDONIA
18 BRECON BEACONS
32 NORTH WALES & SNOWDONIA
34 PEMBROKESHIRE & CARMARTHENSHIRE
41 MID WALES
55 GOWER, SWANSEA & CARDIFF

Short Walks
14 SNOWDONIA
31 BRECON BEACONS

Heart of England
Pathfinder Walks
6 COTSWOLDS
14 SHROPSHIRE & STAFFORDSHIRE
20 SHERWOOD FOREST & THE EAST MIDLANDS
29 WYE VALLEY & FOREST OF DEAN
40 MORE COTSWOLDS
74 THE MALVERNS TO WARWICKSHIRE

Short Walks
4 COTSWOLDS
32 HEREFORDSHIRE & THE WYE VALLEY

East of England
Pathfinder Walks
44 ESSEX
45 NORFOLK
48 SUFFOLK
50 LINCOLNSHIRE & THE WOLDS
51 CAMBRIDGESHIRE & THE FENS

Short Walks
33 NORFOLK INTO SUFFOLK

South West of England
Pathfinder Walks
1 SOUTH DEVON & DARTMOOR
5 CORNWALL
9 EXMOOR & THE QUANTOCKS
11 DORSET & THE JURASSIC COAST
21 SOMERSET, THE MENDIPS & WILTSHIRE
26 DARTMOOR
68 NORTH & MID DEVON
69 SOUTH WEST ENGLAND COASTAL WALKS

Short Walks
8 DARTMOOR
9 CORNWALL
10 SOMERSET FROM BATH TO THE QUANTOCKS
21 EXMOOR
29 SOUTH DEVON

South East of England
Pathfinder Walks
8 KENT
12 NEW FOREST, HAMPSHIRE & SOUTH DOWNS
25 THAMES VALLEY & CHILTERNS
37 LONDON'S PARKS & COUNTRYSIDE
54 HERTFORDSHIRE & BEDFORDSHIRE
65 SURREY
66 WEST SUSSEX & THE SOUTH DOWNS
67 SOUTH DOWNS NATIONAL PARK & EAST SUSSEX
72 COUNTRY WALKS NEAR LONDON

Short Walks
7 THE CHILTERNS
23 NEW FOREST NATIONAL PARK
27 ISLE OF WIGHT

Practical Guides
GPS FOR WALKERS
MAP READING SKILLS